## AMERICAN HISTORY

# Twentieth-Century Immigration to the United States

Stuart A. Kallen

D1259954

**LUCENT BOOKS**
*A part of Gale, Cengage Learning*

GALE
CENGAGE Learning

Detroit • New York • San Francisco • New Haven, Conn • Waterville, Maine • London

© 2007 Lucent Books, a part of Gale, Cengage Learning

For more information, contact
Lucent Books
27500 Drake Rd.
Farmington Hills, MI 48331-3535
Or you can visit our Internet site at http://www.gale.com

LIBRARY OF CONGRESS CATALOGING-IN-PUBLICATION DATA

Kallen, Stuart A., 1955–
Twentieth-century immigration to the United States / by Stuart A. Kallen.
  p. cm. — (American history)
Includes bibliographical references and index.
ISBN-13: 978-1-59018-186-7 (hardcover)
1. United States—Emigration and immigration—History—20th century—Juvenile literature. 2. Immigrants—United States—History—20th century—Juvenile literature. I. Title.
JV6455.K35 2007
304.8'7300904—dc22

2007015977

ISBN-10: 1-59018-186-7

Printed in the United States of America
2 3 4 5 6 7 12 11 10 09 08

# Contents

# Foreword

The United States has existed as a nation for just over two hundred years. By comparison, Rome existed as a nation-state for more than one thousand years. Out of a few struggling British colonies, the United States developed relatively quickly into a world power whose policy decisions and culture have great influence on the world stage. What events and aspirations drove this young American nation to such great heights in such a short period of time? The answer lies in a close study of its varied and unique history. As James Baldwin once remarked, "American history is longer, larger, more various, more beautiful, and more terrible than anything anyone has ever said about it."

The basic facts of United States history—names, dates, places, battles, treaties, speeches, and acts of Congress—fill countless textbooks. These facts, though essential to a thorough understanding of world events, are rarely compelling for students. More compelling are the stories in history, the experience of history.

Titles in this series explore the history of the country and the experiences of Americans. What influences led the colonists to risk everything and break from Britain? Who was the driving force behind the Constitution? Which factors led thousands of people to leave their homelands and settle in the United States? Questions like these do not have simple answers; by discussing them, however, we can view the past as a more real, interesting, and accessible place.

Students will find excellent tools for research and investigation in every title. Lucent Books' American History series provides not only facts, but also the analysis and context necessary for insightful critical thinking about history and about current events. Fully cited quotations from historical figures, eyewitnesses, letters, speeches, and writings bring vibrancy and authority to the text. Annotated bibliographies allow students to evaluate and locate sources for further investigation. Sidebars highlight important and interesting figures, events, or related primary source excerpts. Timelines, maps, and full color images add another dimension of accessibility to the stories being told.

It has been said the past has a history of repeating itself, for good and ill. In these pages, students will learn a bit about both and, perhaps, better understand their own place in this world.

# Important Dates at the Time of Twentieth-

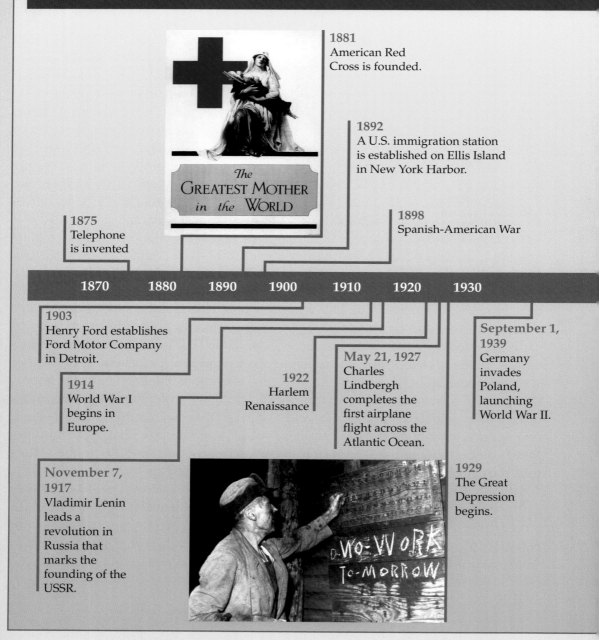

**1881**
American Red Cross is founded.

**1892**
A U.S. immigration station is established on Ellis Island in New York Harbor.

**1898**
Spanish-American War

**1875**
Telephone is invented

| 1870 | 1880 | 1890 | 1900 | 1910 | 1920 | 1930 |

**1903**
Henry Ford establishes Ford Motor Company in Detroit.

**1914**
World War I begins in Europe.

**1922**
Harlem Renaissance

**May 21, 1927**
Charles Lindbergh completes the first airplane flight across the Atlantic Ocean.

**September 1, 1939**
Germany invades Poland, launching World War II.

**November 7, 1917**
Vladimir Lenin leads a revolution in Russia that marks the founding of the USSR.

**1929**
The Great Depression begins.

**1979–80**
52 Americans
are held
hostage in Iran.

**1963**
President John
F. Kennedy is
assassinated.

**January 1, 1983**
The first Internet
network is
established by the
National Science
Foundation.

| 1940 | 1950 | 1960 | 1970 | 1980 | 1990 | 2000 | 2010 |
|------|------|------|------|------|------|------|------|

**1989**
The Berlin Wall falls
in Germany.

**January 1,
1994**
The North
American
Free Trade
Agreement
(NAFTA)
goes into
effect.

**2001**
Terrorists attack the
World Trade Center
and the Pentagon.

**2003**
U.S. declares war on
Iraq.

# Modern Immigration: Benefit or Burden?

In the nineties the debate over immigration was clear. One side argued that foreign invaders were taking American jobs. Newspaper columnists declared the United States full and claimed that the nation could not accept more people. The majority of Americans believed it was not their responsibility to help foreigners from impoverished lands. Many citizens also expressed widespread resentment of immigrants who refused to learn English, adopt cherished American customs, or otherwise assimilate into mainstream American society.

Those who favored immigration countered that the United States needed immigrants to work at menial jobs shunned by Americans. They also argued that the diversity provided by immigrants helped make America a stronger nation.

So went the national debate in the nineties—the 1890s. The debate over immigration in the United States at the beginning of the twentieth century sounded much like the debate grabbing headlines in the 1990s, a hundred years later. In the 1890s the controversy focused on immigrants from southern and eastern Europe, in the 1990s from Latin America, but the issues were very similar. Indeed, the same arguments had been made in the 1790s, when debate arose over Irish and German immigrants.

Immigration has been a concern in the United States since the nation was founded. But only in the late 1800s did the U.S. government attempt to regulate immigration by law. The century of immigration controls that followed, sometimes blocking and sometimes welcoming immigration, profoundly shaped U.S. society and reflects one of the most divisive issues in U.S. history.

## "Convicts, Lunatics, Idiots"

Before 1882 anyone could move to the United States. But as the population grew, established residents began to call for immigration regulation to protect the racial, religious, and ethnic heritage of the United States. Between 1850 and 1880 some three hundred thousand Chinese people had come to the United States, many to work as laborers on massive westward expansion projects like the transcontinental railroad. This first wave of Asian immigrants looked very different from the majority population of European ancestry and minority of African Americans, and the Chinese faced bitter discrimination. As Maldwyn Allen Jones writes in *American Immigration:* "It was . . . widely believed that the Chinese were an inassimilable, even subversive group, and that their . . . customs and habits were a social menace."[1]

Responding to widespread anti-immigrant sentiment, Congress passed the first immigration law. Called the Chinese Exclusion Act of 1882, the law barred all immigration from China. The Chinese Exclusion Act also limited immigration by people from any nation considered undesirable at the time. In the words of the act, officials could bar entry to those who were "convicts, lunatics, idiots, and persons likely to become public charges."[2]

The Chinese Exclusion Act did little to control the main source of U.S. immigra-

*New immigrants to America crowd the deck of the ship S.S.* Prince Frederick Wilhelm *in 1915.*

tion. Between 1880 and 1900, 9 million immigrants arrived on American shores, mostly from Italy, Austria-Hungary, and Russia. Many of these immigrants were escaping war, famine, and religious persecution, and most were poor. Rumors of wealth in the United States drew millions to leave Europe behind. As Lithuanian immigrant Pauline Newman, who moved to the United States in the early twentieth century, states: "America was known to foreigners as the land where you'd get rich. There's gold on the sidewalk—all you have to do is pick it up. So people left [their] little village and went to America."[3]

They quickly discovered the streets were not paved with gold. Instead they found poverty, low-wage jobs, and squalid living conditions. They also faced prejudice. Many of the immigrants were Catholic or Jewish and their presence was opposed by people who believed America's Protestant heritage was threatened. Among those who felt this way were powerful business leaders, politicians, and religious figures. They had a strong influence over governmental affairs and repeatedly introduced legislation to limit immigration.

## The Immigration Act

Until the 1890s immigration laws were enacted and enforced by individual states. But in 1891 immigration opponents finally convinced the federal government to take control of the situation. Congress passed the Immigration Act of 1891, which created the Office of Immigration within the U.S. Treasury Department. The law charged the federal government with "inspecting, admitting, rejecting, and processing all immigrants seeking admission to the United States."[4]

The Office of Immigration immediately created rules to bar certain classes of people. In the parlance of the day, these people included "polygamists, persons convicted of crimes of moral turpitude, and those suffering loathsome or contagious diseases."[5] Thus, though this early law did not exclude Europeans on the basis of national origin, millions of European immigrants were refused entry into the United States because they were sick or thought to be immoral.

## Huddled Masses

In the early years of the twentieth century, the number of legal restrictions against immigrants continued to grow. Finally, after World War I (1914–1918), Congress severely restricted all immigration to the United States. However, stories about the freedom and opportunities afforded to U.S. residents continued to resonate around the world. When Congress eased restrictions in 1965, immigration rose sharply and soon millions were arriving each year. Many were inspired by the promise of America famously inscribed on the Statue of Liberty in New York Harbor: "Give me your tired, your poor, Your huddled masses yearning to breathe free, The wretched refuse of your teeming shore. Send these, the homeless, tempest-tost to me, I lift my lamp beside the golden door!"[6]

The noble ideals expressed by Russian immigrant Emma Lazarus do not reflect the discord and challenges that U.S. immigrants actually faced. Throughout the twentieth century—and into the twenty-first—Americans have waged heated debates about the poor, homeless, tempest-tost immigrants arriving on their shores. With the population of the country growing by nearly 400 percent since 1900, there is little doubt that this debate will continue into the future.

# Chapter One

# The Ellis Island Years

Congress passed the Immigration Act of 1891 to screen the continuous flow of humanity arriving on American shores in the late 1800s. To do so, the act created the Office of the Superintendent of Immigration. This federal bureau oversaw a newly created corps called the U.S. Immigrant Inspectors, which processed immigrants in several major American cities including Philadelphia, Boston, and San Francisco.

The vast majority of immigrants, however—three-quarters of all new arrivals—landed in New York City. So the government decided to post immigration inspectors at the port of New York in a new facility designed to process immigrants on a mass scale. This center, known as Ellis Island, would come to symbolize the promise and problems of twentieth-century U.S. immigration.

## "Europe's Unwashed Masses"

The federal immigration station was built on Ellis Island, a 3.3-acre (1.3ha) dot of land in the mouth of the Hudson River in New York Harbor. The government originally wanted to construct the processing facility on nearby Liberty Island, home of the Statue of Liberty. This site was rejected, however, as Virginia Yans-McLaughlin and Marjorie Lightman explain in *Ellis Island and the Peopling of America*: "[Many] native-born Americans thought the symbol of liberty might be tainted by the daily passage of thousands of Europe's unwashed masses."[7]

The station at Ellis Island opened on January 1, 1892. The next day, Annie Moore, a fifteen-year-old Irish girl, entered the history books as the first person processed in the center. It was immediately apparent that the center would get all the volume it could handle. By the mid-1890s inspectors were processing up to five thousand immigrants every day—about two people per minute.

However, on June 14, 1897, a mysterious fire burned the wooden immigration structure to the ground. Although no one was injured, millions of state and federal records were lost in the fire. The Treasury Department immediately began construction of a new facility, this one fireproof. Until it could be completed, immigrants were processed at the New York State immigration facilities in Manhattan, which had been in use from 1855 to the 1890s, before Ellis Island was opened. On December 17, 1900, the new Main Building on Ellis Island was opened and 2,251 immigrants were received that day. Until 1913 an average of about a million immigrants a year were processed at Ellis Island.

## The Atmosphere in Steerage

Most immigrants arrived on Ellis Island frightened and hungry, and many who were healthy when they started their gru-

eling voyage across the Atlantic were sick by the time they reached New York. About 90 percent of all immigrants traveled in steerage, or third class. People in this cheapest category were crowded together near the bottom of the ship and most were seasick during the entire two- to three-week journey. A report by the federal government describes the appalling conditions in steerage:

The ventilation is almost always inadequate, and the air soon becomes foul. The unattended vomit of the seasick, the odors of not too clean bodies, the reek of food and the awful stench of the nearby toilet rooms make the atmosphere of the steerage such that it is a marvel that human flesh can endure it. . . . Most

*Millions of immigrants passed through the immigration processing center at Ellis Island between 1892 and 1954.*

# The Old World Meets the New

*Most immigrants from small villages were completely unprepared to pass through Ellis Island. Italian immigrant Bianca De Carli describes the travails of a Hungarian woman she met aboard a ship in 1913:*

One woman had sewed her papers and money . . . into the folds of her seventeen skirts! Yes, seventeen. . . . She came from a Hungarian . . . [province] and she told me that a woman's wealth was proved by the number of skirts she could wear. Well, that afternoon when we could see the land . . . a steamship man told us all to check our papers . . . and have everything ready. . . .

Well, this skirt lady I was telling you about started to cry and wail. . . . [She] thought she would not have time to cut the hundreds of threads which held those little paper monies into her skirts. Another lady had a lot of sewing scissors and a little blade, and so about five of us divided the skirts and we went over every inch of them—they had lots of folds and when spread out were very wide—and put what we found each in a little pile. . . . When she was sure that no one in America cared how many skirts she had . . . she wore only two through the examination and carried the others in a big bundle!

Quoted in Willard A. Heaps, *The Story of Ellis Island*. New York: Seabury, 1967, pp. 49–50.

immigrants lie in their berths for most of the voyage, in a stupor caused by the foul air. The food often repels them. . . . It is almost impossible to keep personally clean. All of these conditions are naturally aggravated by the crowding.[8]

Upon arrival all immigrants had to pass a medical examination before they were allowed entry into the United States. This was usually not a problem for a ship's first- and second-class passengers, who paid more for their tickets. These passengers typically passed a cursory inspection by health officials at the landing docks

and directly entered the country. However, people with third-class tickets were transported from the landing docks to Ellis Island, where they faced a barrage of more thorough inspections that were humiliating and frightening.

## Inspections and Rejections

Most who passed through Ellis Island would never forget the experience. Upon arriving at the island, passengers walked single-file up the grand staircase in the Great Hall. As they climbed the stairs medical officers watched closely, looking for weakness and disability. This process is described on the Ellis Island Web site:

The inspections took place in the Registry Room (or Great Hall), where doctors would briefly scan every immigrant for obvious physical ailments. Doctors at Ellis Island soon became very adept at conducting these "six second physicals." By 1916, it was said that a doctor could identify numerous medical conditions (ranging from anemia to goiters to varicose veins) just by glancing at an immigrant.[9]

During this physical survey, immigrants identified with potential medical problems were marked on the front right shoulder of their garments. Those labeled with an X were suspected of general mental problems. If the X was circled, a definite problem had been observed. Others were marked for possible physical infirmities: B indicated a bad back, C conjunctivitis, Ft bad feet, G goiter, H heart, K hernia, P lungs, and S senility. Marked individuals were ordered to submit to a secondary, more thorough examination by a doctor in a private room.

Those marked CT were treated to a rather bizarre examination. CT indicated trachoma, a highly contagious eye disease that can cause blindness. It was feared that people with this affliction would become public charges, so inspectors particularly scrutinized arrivals for possible cases of trachoma. To check for the disease, doctors peeled back the eyelids with a metal buttonhook. People with redness, discharges, and other telltale symptoms were deported. So common was this disease that about half of all immigrants who were refused entry for medical reasons had a CT marked on their coat.

Ellis Island doctors routinely checked six other areas: the scalp, face, neck, hands, gait, and general condition. These examinations sometimes revealed deadly infectious diseases, including cholera, malaria, smallpox, measles, and yellow fever. Immigrants could also be barred from entry for much more vague conditions collectively called "loathsome." Immigration law categorized these as diseases "which excite abhorrence and loathing by reason of the knowledge of their existence."[10] The loathsome diseases were often disfiguring. For example, a type of ringworm called favus, which caused unsightly yellow scabs and baldness, was considered a loathsome disease that disqualified an immigrant from entry.

*On Ellis Island, immigrant children are checked for diseases in 1911.*

## Mental Tests

Because federal legislation prevented people then called "idiots, imbeciles, and morons"[11] from entering the country, immigrants were given intelligence tests at Ellis Island. Such tests, which might consist of word games or jigsaw puzzles, were brief and unsophisticated, and determinations of intelligence were not scientific. Often language and cultural barriers between inspectors and new arrivals bewildered test subjects who were already nervous, tired, and confused. There were humorous moments amid the stress, however. As Yans-McLaughlin and Lightman write, one inspector asked a woman, "Would you wash stairs from the top down or from the bottom up?" She replied indignantly, "I didn't come to America to wash stairs."[12] That woman passed her test.

Immigrants who failed to pass mental or physical tests were separated from panicked friends and relatives and detained for further testing. Those who were obviously sick with some common ailments, such as whooping cough or diphtheria, were sent to hospital wards and treated. Most were allowed to enter the country when their health improved.

Only 2 percent of immigrants were refused entry into the United States. Nevertheless, that represented a significant number of would-be immigrants, about twenty thousand people a year. Some who were deported never saw their spouses, children, or other relatives again. If a child was refused entry, the entire family had to return to their port of origin since children were not allowed to travel alone. For this reason Ellis Island was known by some as the "Isle of Tears" or "Heartbreak Island."

*A Greek family arrives with all their belongings at Ellis Island in 1925.*

# Legal Inspection

During the early 1900s many immigrants had to pass another, totally subjective test before they were allowed to enter the United States. Fears of foreign revolutionaries, Communists, and adherents of other ideologies associated with anarchy or foreigners were widespread at the time, so some arrivals faced what was called a legal inspection. This was meant to screen out polygamists, anarchists, and others seen as undesirable based on their political or religious beliefs. Subjects enduring legal inspection had to prove that they had high moral character and had come to the United States for acceptable reasons.

Women faced particular discrimination during the legal inspection. They were automatically refused entry, for example, if it was determined they were unwed mothers. Women often were detained for legal inspection simply for being unaccompanied—inspectors rarely checked first to see if she was a widow, married to a man who was not present, or in the company of her legitimate children.

Those who failed the legal inspection were segregated by gender and detained in huge dormitories. Usually, if relatives came forward who could vouch for and take responsibility for them, they were released. Otherwise, the detainees were ordered to appear for further questioning at a Board of Special Inquiry made up of three people appointed by the commissioner of immigration. The board did not offer immigrants the same civil rights granted in a regular U.S. court. Its decisions were arbitrary; if the board determined someone was a criminal, an immoral character, or likely to become a financial burden on the public, he or she was deported and the decision could not be appealed.

For most immigrants, the Ellis Island experience only lasted a few hours. When it was over, they were free to enter the United States. Until 1921 there were no visas, passports, birth certificates, or other proof of identification or official documents required.

# Tenements and Sweatshops

Between 1900 and 1920 large numbers of Europeans arrived in the United States. They included more than 2 million Italians, 2.4 million eastern European Jews, and about 1.5 million Poles. Many never traveled far beyond Ellis Island, settling where they first set foot in New York, one of the richest cities in the world.

Many Italian and Jewish immigrants established ethnic communities in Manhattan's Lower East Side neighborhoods, where rents were cheap, landlords would rent to newcomers, and one could find comfort in familiar languages and customs. Work was also available on the Lower East Side, largely in sweatshops where the new Americans toiled twelve hours a day, six days a week for less than a dollar a day. Those who labored in these factories ranged in age from eight to eighty years old.

Work dominated immigrant life. Outside work, recent immigrants mainly lived in densely packed apartments called tenements. Conditions in these run-down buildings were not much different than those found in steerage aboard a

*Many early immigrants lived in tenement-style neighborhoods like the one pictured here on the Lower East Side section of New York City.*

steamship. Dozens of people shared a common bathroom and large families lived in one or two tiny rooms. Disease was rampant, promoted by unsanitary conditions vividly described in the *New York Times*:

The chief objections to the old-style tenements are . . . lack of family privacy, and promiscuous toilet arrangements, inviting moral deterioration; lack of light and air, and of sanitary accommodations, insuring a large death rate, and danger from fire—that ever-present tenement horror. All of these are wickedly cruel when such houses are new; when they become old, dilapidated, infested with vermin and infected with disease germs, they are a disgrace to humanity and a menace, not only to the health of the unfortunate residents therein, but to the health of the whole community.[13]

The advantages of ethnic communities offset the poverty of tenement life. For example, Jews on the Lower East Side lived among others who spoke the Yiddish dialect of their homeland. They were close to synagogues, kosher food stores, dozens of Yiddish theaters, and friends and family from the old country. American Jews were also able to practice their religious traditions openly, something they had been denied for centuries in most of Europe.

## Filling Up America

While New York was the final destination for many, others fanned out across the Midwest after leaving Ellis Island. Many were moving to cities where other family members had earlier established residence. For example, it was not unusual for several men in a family to move to a city, get jobs, rent an apartment, and then send for their wives, sisters, mothers, and grandmothers back in their native country. This was the case for millions of immigrants who settled in Chicago, Cleveland, Detroit, and Milwaukee, the industrial centers of the early twentieth century.

The Midwest was a magnet for immigrants during a time of unparalleled industrial expansion in the United States. Henry Ford established Ford Motor Company in Detroit in 1903 and unskilled workers came from all over the world to build Ford's Model T automobile, produced with assembly-line technology that was soon

# Life in a New York Sweatshop

*In 1905 thirteen-year-old orphaned Polish immigrant Sadie Frowne described her work in a garment factory in New York City:*

At seven o'clock we all sit down to our machines and the boss brings to each one the pile of work that he or she is to finish during the day. . . . Sometimes the work is not all finished by six o'clock and then the one who is behind must work overtime. . . .

The machines go like mad all day, because the faster you work the more money you get. Sometimes in my haste I get my finger caught and the needle goes right through it. . . . I bind the finger up with a piece of cotton and go on working. We all have accidents like that. Where the needle goes through the nail . . . or where it splinters a bone it does much harm. Sometimes a finger has to come off. . . . So we have to be careful as well as swift. But I am getting so good at the work that within a year I will be making $7 a week, and then I can save at least $3.50 a week. I have over $200 saved now.

Sadie Frowne, "Immigrating to America, 1905," *EyeWitness to History, 2005.* www.eyewitnesstohistory.com.

adopted by industries across the country. General Motors, founded in Flint, Michigan, in 1908, was also a popular destination for immigrant laborers. The growing automakers used large quantities of steel produced in Cleveland, Buffalo, Gary, and Pittsburgh. Like New York and Detroit, these cities quickly filled with unskilled European immigrants seeking factory work.

Chicago was a leading agricultural center with the world's largest rail hub and the nation's busiest ports. The Chicago Union Stockyards dominated the meatpacking industy and attracted European immigrants by the thousands. Between the late 1880s and the early 1900s, the population of Chicago swelled from about 300,000 to 1.7 million, making it one of the fastest-growing cities in world history.

The factory jobs taken by immigrants were grueling—workweeks were ninety hours and pay was only $5 to $10 a month (the equivalent of $150–$300 per month in 2006). However, a dozen eggs at the time cost 14 cents and a small house cost around $2,000. Millions of immigrant families found that if they lived frugally and worked hard, their dream of eventually owning a car, a house, and even their own business was within reach. These achievements would have been impossible had they remained in the poverty-scarred Italian countryside or continued to endure persecution in the Jewish ghettos of

*Workers assemble a Ford Model T automobile in Highland Park, Michigan, 1913.*

Poland and Russia, so immigrant Americans worked and saved and, for the most part, did not complain.

## A Growing Backlash

The exodus from Europe during the early 1900s may have put the American Dream within reach for millions of new immigrants, but it created a growing backlash in the United States among native-born Americans, called nativists (themselves descendants of immigrants, not of Native American Indians).

Most nativists identified themselves as Anglo-Saxons, people who could trace their heritage to northern European nations such as Great Britain, Scotland, and the Scandinavian countries. Nativist Anglo-Saxons were primarily Protestant and light-skinned. Many held anti-Catholic and anti-Semitic views, and some openly argued the superiority of the blond-haired, blue-eyed white race, as distinguished from darker-skinned southern and eastern Europeans. These feelings were put into words by author Jack London, widely known for his 1903 bestseller *Call of the Wild.* In 1913 London wrote several novels that criticized new immigrants, calling them "the dark-pigmented things, the half-castes, the mongrel-bloods of southern and eastern Europe"[14] who diluted the racial "purity" of the immigrant groups that founded the United States.

A word commonly used to describe nativists is xenophobic, those who are unduly fearful and contemptuous of foreigners. While most Americans were not xenophobes, the nativists were well organized and politically powerful. They formed dozens of organizations with names like the Immigration Restriction League and the Order of United Americans. These groups included representatives in Congress as well as mayors, sheriffs, and other local politicians. And they lobbied hard for Congress to restrict the number of immigrants allowed into the United States.

## Backlash and Restrictions

The first immigration restrictions of the twentieth century were passed in 1903, purportedly as a reaction to the assassination of President William McKinley in September 1901. McKinley was shot by an anarchist named Leon Czolgosz, an American of Polish-Russian descent. Anti-immigrant forces capitalized on public anger in the aftermath of the assassination to rally support for laws preventing anarchists from migrating to the United States.

In 1907 immigrant exclusions were further broadened to include, in the language of the time, imbeciles, the feeble-minded, tuberculars, epileptics, professional beggars, persons with physical or mental defects, and persons under age sixteen without parents. Finally, in 1917, after a twenty-two-year effort by select members of Congress, a literacy test was introduced. All immigrants sixteen years of age or older were required to demonstrate the ability to read a forty-word passage in their native language as part of the new-arrival inspection process. Individuals were given a holy book in their native language and ordered to read aloud: Christians read from the New Testament of the Bible, Jews the Torah, and Muslims the Koran. Illiteracy was grounds for deportation.

# The Campaign Against Hyphenated Americans

*In 1915 as World War I raged in Europe , former president Theodore Roosevelt spoke strongly against European nationalism and what he called hyphenated Americans in a widely circulated speech excerpted below:*

The one absolutely certain way of bringing this nation to ruin, of preventing all possibility of its continuing to be a nation at all, would be to permit it to become a tangle of squabbling nationalities, an intricate knot of German-Americans, Irish-Americans, English-Americans, French-Americans, Scandinavian-Americans or Italian- Americans, each preserving its separate nationality, each at heart feeling more sympathy with Europeans of that nationality, than with the other citizens of the American Republic. The men who do not become Americans and nothing else are hyphenated Americans; and there ought to be no room for them in this country. . . . He has no place here; and the sooner he returns to the land to which he feels his real heart-allegiance, the better it will be for every good American. There is no such thing as a hyphenated American who is a good American. . . .

For an American citizen to vote as a German-American . . . is to be a traitor to American institutions; and those hyphenated Americans who terrorize American politicians by threats of the foreign vote are engaged in treason to the American Republic.

Theodore Roosevelt, "Theodore Roosevelt Advocates Americanism, 1915," *Proud to Be an American,* 2002. www.rpatrick.com/USA/americanism.

Meanwhile, as the federal government was creating barriers to immigration, state governments were passing discriminatory laws to prevent foreign competition in certain trades. For example, Michigan legislators sought to limit the number of Italian hair cutters by denying barber licenses to non-Americans. Other states prevented aliens from practicing trades associated with law, medicine, accounting, architecture, engineering, and surveying.

Some states passed laws that bordered on the absurd. Massachusetts, for example, made it a crime for non-Americans to pick wild berries or wildflowers from public lands. Pennsylvania sought to limit foreign competition to hunters by prohibiting immigrants from obtaining hunting licenses or owning hunting dogs and shotguns.

## Moving South and West

Facing restrictions and discrimination in the East and Midwest, a small percentage of immigrants chose to relocate. Thousands of Italian, Portuguese, and Slavic people made their way to communities in the South and West Coast to work as miners, fishermen, farmers, and railroad and construction workers. However, some found a violent strain of anti-alien nativism worse than what they left behind. As John Higham writes in *Strangers in the Land:*

> The South and the Pacific Coast alike thought of themselves as a "white man's country." They had long struggled—in different ways—to maintain white supremacy . . . . From Seattle to Savannah primitive race feelings, wrought deeply in the American character, flourished as nowhere else in the United States. Projected onto the new immigration, these ancient feelings gave southern and western nativism its peculiar energy.[15]

## Anti-Asian Hysteria

In California nativist aggression was directed at Japanese immigrants, another Asian minority targeted much as Chinese immigrants had been in the late 1800s. Anti-Japanese sentiment was aggravated

*Japanese immigrant children in 1920. Immigrants of many nationalities experienced racism from the "nativist" or native-born Americans of the early twentieth century.*

by the growing military power of Japan, which had evicted Russia from some contested islands in 1905 and started a war between the two countries. The Russo-Japanese War sparked near-hysteria in California, where some feared a secret invasion of what was called the "Yellow Peril." A novel by military scholar Homer Lea, *The Valor of Ignorance,* fed these fears: Lea's book was a detailed, though fictional, account of a Japanese takeover of California by average-looking citizens who were really undercover soldiers and spies.

The Yellow Peril panic spread to the California statehouse and in 1905 the legislature unanimously approved a bill that called a halt to all Japanese immigration. It also approved segregating Japanese students in schools. The same year, one hundred thousand people joined the newly formed Asiatic Exclusion League, which organized a boycott of all Japanese-American businesses.

In 1907, reacting to the prevailing political climate, President Theodore Roosevelt negotiated an agreement with Japan, promising to desegregate California schools. In return, the Japanese government pledged to stop the emigration of its citizens to the United States.

## Scientific Racism

Many who opposed Japanese immigration based their racism on a pseudo-scientific movement called eugenics that was popular at the time. Eugenics supporters divided human beings into biological types based on culture. Members of different cultures were believed to have unique physical and emotional character-istics that were unchangeable and undeniable, and adherents ranked cultures in a racist hierarchy. As Jones explains:

[Eugenics] warned against the consequences of breeding from inferior stock. In the United States, where the eugenics movement enjoyed a remarkable vogue . . . its teachings were eagerly seized upon by upper-class nativists already concerned for the survival of the Anglo-Saxon stock and haunted by fears of "race suicide" [dilution of racial bloodlines through intermarriage]. Thus about 1906 the Boston intellectuals who directed the Immigration Restriction League began to point to genetic principles as a scientific basis for their claim that immigrating restriction was essential to preserve American racial purity.[16]

The beliefs of the eugenicists were based on the writings of William Z. Ripley. His book, *Races of Europe,* divided Europeans into the desirable northern Teutons and the undesirable central Alpines and Mediterraneans.

Ripley inspired wealthy New York nativist Madison Grant to write his own book, *The Passing of the Great Race in America,* in 1916. Grant called for immigration officials to ban Alpines, Mediterraneans, and Jews to preserve the Anglo-Saxon culture. Unless this was done, Grant wrote, "the great race . . . [of American] soldiers, sailors, adventurers, explorers, rulers, organizers and aristocrats [will be replaced by] the weak, the broken and the mentally crippled of all races."[17]

## Campaign Against German Americans

In addition to eugenic principles, American nativists drew upon a hodgepodge of ideologies to justify and spread fear of foreigners. In New England nativism was driven by lofty pseudoscientific reasoning; in the South it was based on entrenched racism against African Americans; and in the West xenophobes were motivated by overblown paranoia of Asian invasion.

Whatever ideology was behind nativist thinking, xenophobia swept across the nation when World War I erupted in Europe in 1914. At first the United States tried to remain neutral in the conflict. However, in 1915, a German submarine torpedoed the British ocean liner *Lusitania,* killing twelve hundred people, including several prominent Americans. This brutal attack on innocent civilians galvanized American opinion against Germans and German immigrants in the United States, spawning a movement called "100 per cent Americanism."

Those who subscribed to the Americanism movement believed that many German Americans remained loyal to German leader Kaiser Wilhelm II. This led to a campaign against "hyphenated" Americans, especially German Americans, led by former president Theodore Roosevelt, who proclaimed:

> There is no room in this country for hyphenated Americanism. . . . [A] hyphenated American is not an American at all. . . . Americanism is a matter of the spirit and of the soul. Our allegiance must be purely to the United States. We must unsparingly condemn any man who holds any other allegiance. . . . The foreign-born population of this country must be an Americanized population—no other kind can fight the battles of America either in war or peace. It must talk the language of its native-born fellow-citizens, it must possess American citizenship and American ideals. It must stand firm by its oath of allegiance in word and deed and must show that in very fact it has renounced allegiance to every prince, potentate, or foreign government.[18]

*Former president Theodore Roosevelt led a campaign against so-called "hyphenated" Americans, with German Americans being the main target.*

*Hundreds of immigrants await processing in the Great Hall of Ellis Island in this undated photo.*

Roosevelt's rhetoric helped promote anti-German hysteria across the country. Although there were no cases of disloyalty by German Americans, rumors of immigrant spies and saboteurs were widely circulated.

## War Against German Immigrants

After the United States entered World War I against Germany, Austria-Hungary, and the Turks in 1917, nativists engaged in an all-out war on German immigrants and their culture. States passed laws that forbade the teaching of the German language in schools and Henry Ford established a compulsory English school for his foreign-born workers.

German cultural icons were also targeted. Music by German composers such as Beethoven and Bach was banned from performance by symphony orchestras. Statues of German writers Johann Wolfgang von Goethe and Friedrich Schiller were vandalized or removed from parks.

Towns with German-sounding names were renamed. Germantown, Nebraska, for example, became Garland and Berlin, Iowa, was renamed Lincoln. Food names were also transformed: Sauerkraut came to be called liberty cabbage and hamburgers were renamed Salisbury steaks. In Massachusetts, a physician even changed the name of German measles to "liberty" measles.

The anti-German sentiment spawned widespread violence. In Idaho German American farmers were tarred and feathered. In Florida and California, German Americans were publicly flogged. In Illinois, Robert Prager, a German immigrant, was lynched in 1918.

## End of an Era

The treatment of German immigrants during World War I was an outgrowth of nativism that had periodically gripped Americans since the founding of the nation. Like previous debates over immigration, the opposition was driven by major world events that had little to do with daily life in America. However, the end of World War I in 1918 did not mean anti-immigrant sentiment would subside.

After decades of nearly unrestricted immigration, Americans were ready after World War I to stop, or at least restrict, immigration. Nativist sentiment would influence immigration policy for the next fifty years. The image of Ellis Island, and of nearly unrestricted immigration, would live on in the national imagination, but the reality would be the closing of the open door and serious attempts to lock it tightly.

# Chapter Two

# Closing the Doors

B y 1918 Americans were feeling the effects of one of the largest human migrations in history. In the previous decades, millions had left Europe and moved to the United States, changing the face of the country. In most big cities, ethnic neighborhoods grew up, filled with Italians, Irish, Jews, Poles, Slavs, Armenians, Russians, Greeks, and a host of smaller ethnic groups. Foods, music, art, literature, entertainment, and religious practices from the old country were added to the mix of established Anglo-Saxon traditions, and urban American culture developed a more international character that had yet to reach much of rural America.

The post–World War I years were also a time of unprecedented economic prosperity in the United States. The war had destroyed the European economy and fragmented Europe politically, but the United States had escaped physical damage. Despite the nation's strength, the war had damaged public attitudes, however; war-weary Americans retained a pervasive dread of all things European that led to isolationism and a new era of severely restricted immigration.

## Revolutions and Reds

Americans were extremely wary of Europeans for several reasons. First, the European powers were blamed for the untold suffering and destruction of the war, which had cost more than a hundred thousand Americans' lives. Second, many Americans feared the political instability in war-torn Europe would spread to the United States. In particular, a radical new political ideology, communism, developed by German philosopher Karl Marx, was taking hold in eastern Europe. In March 1917 a revolution toppled the repressive imperial government of Czar Nicholas II in Russia. The monarchy was replaced by a government led by Vladimir Ilyich Ulyanov, known as Lenin, the leader of the Russian Communist, or Bolshevik, Party.

According to communist theory, a nation's property and wealth belonged to all members of society and everyone, from factory workers to the leaders of the nation, were equals, or of the same class. Communists criticized the American capitalist system because they believed a few wealthy business owners controlled vast amounts of wealth and power while forcing laborers to work long hours for little pay. Lenin openly stated that he wanted to overthrow capitalism and spread communism to the workers of the world under the red flag of the Soviet Union.

Many nativists viewed communism and socialism, both of which opposed private ownership of property and elite classes of wealthy people, as a direct threat to the American way of life. Likewise, they viewed supporters of principles or policies that challenged the capitalist status quo as

dangerous subversives. Americans who agitated for equal rights were suspected as a potential source of this workers' revolution because they demonstrated for better working conditions, higher wages, and a more equitable society. Although most continued to support capitalism, these agitators were often labeled Soviets, Bolsheviks, Communists, and Reds. This was particularly true for members of organized labor unions, many of whom had immigrated to the United States from eastern Europe before World War I. These immigrant agitators were often at odds with the capitalist Anglo-Saxon owners of America's leading industrial corporations.

## Strikes and Strife

Labor unions had been gaining power throughout the early decades of the century. During World War I, as millions of

*Thousands of steel mill workers went on strike in 1919 to fight for higher wages and shorter working hours.*

men were drafted to fight overseas, a labor shortage threatened to cripple industries vital to the war effort. Whereas the auto, steel, rubber, mining, and shipbuilding industries had previously had surpluses of unskilled immigrant workers, the war severely cut the number of immigrants and the existing labor pool. With fewer available laborers to perform necessary tasks, workers were in a position to agitate for shorter work hours and higher wages, and in an even better position when they were organized into unions.

After the war, when returning soldiers eased the labor shortage, company owners began to suppress the unions. This led to widespread unrest, labor strikes, and in a few isolated cases, bombings, riots, and other violence.

The first major postwar strikes occurred in the garment industry immediately after the war when thousands of textile workers went on strike in New York, Massachusetts, Delaware, and elsewhere. The largest strike began in Seattle in January 1919 when more than thirty-five thousand shipyard workers walked off the job after their demands for higher wages were denied. Several weeks later they were joined by thirty thousand other unionized Seattle workers in a general strike.

# Anti-Immigrant Hatred

*By the early 1920s nativists throughout the United States were calling for the widespread deportation of immigrants. John Higham describes their sentiments in* Strangers in the Land:

[The] clamor of the [nativists] . . . rose to an hysterical howl. "Nothing will save the life of this free Republic if these foreign leeches are not cut and cast out," said Mrs. George Thacher Guernsey, president-general of the Daughters of the American Revolution.

Patriotic, veteran, and fraternal organizations demanded more vigorous federal action and sterner legislation. The Farmers National Congress recommended to the United States Justice Department: "burn a brand in the hide of those fellows when you deport them so that if they ever dare return the trade mark will tell its tale and expose them." When the question arose as to where deportees could be sent, one Senator suggested that the North Pole would be a good place. "I do not care where they go, so they get out of here," he said. At the annual picnic of the North Dakota Association of Southern California a speaker advised: "These murderous wild beasts of our otherwise blessed republic should be given a bottle of water and a pint of meal and shoved out into the ocean on a raft, when the wind is blowing seaward."

John Higham, *Strangers in the Land*. New York: Atheneum, 1981, pp. 227–28.

Labor strife continued throughout the year. In May coal miners went on strike in Pennsylvania. In September two hundred fifty thousand steelworkers paralyzed the nation's steel industry, walking off the job in Illinois, Indiana, Ohio, New York, Pennsylvania, and elsewhere. Meanwhile, workers in Dearborn, Michigan, were agitating for union representation, shutting down Ford Motor Company on six separate occasions.

The strikes were largely unsuccessful but strikers were promptly labeled Bolsheviks, Reds, and Communists by the press, politicians, and business owners. Henry Ford linked immigrants and Communists to his own labor troubles in a 1920 editorial in the *Dearborn Independent:*

> There are more Communists in the United States than there are in Soviet Russia. Their aim is the same and their racial character is the same. . . . The power house of Communist influence and propaganda in the United States is in the . . . trade unions which, almost without exception, adhere to a Bolshevik program for the respective industries and for the country as a whole.[19]

## Socialists, Communists, and Anarchists

Despite Ford's accusations, the majority of labor agitators were simply workers who were trying to achieve a better life. Their efforts eventually resulted in gains for American workers that included the forty-hour workweek, overtime pay, and higher wages. However, public fears were not entirely unwarranted. There were avowed, active socialists, Communists, and anarchists in the United States in the 1920s. They were responsible for publishing about fifty incendiary newspapers throughout the country. Some were even plotting a revolution similar to the one carried out by the Bolsheviks in Russia. Many members of radical political groups were immigrants, and their activities put all recent immigrants under a cloud of suspicion.

While the revolutionaries probably never numbered more than several thousand, their tactics frightened many. For example, in Philadelphia in late 1918, anarchists set off bombs outside the homes of two well-known judges and the superintendent of police. No one was injured but periodic attacks on public officials continued for several years.

The strikes, bombings, and outspoken support of the Bolshevik revolution made headlines across the nation. Business leaders mounted a counteroffensive, running ads and giving interviews alleging that immigrants were in the process of mounting a revolution in America. Some factory owners fired all workers who were of Jewish, Russian, or German heritage. Others encouraged their native-born workers to beat up immigrant coworkers who were perceived as Communists when they tried to preach socialism, unionism, or anarchy. Factories also hired vigilante groups to break up strikes and union rallies, still considered hotbeds of Communist activities. Union supporters were beaten, shot, and stabbed.

# The Red Scare

The postwar labor strife was blamed squarely on radical immigrants, as John Higham writes:

> [There] was an impression that radicalism permeated the foreign-born population, that it flourished among immigrants generally and appealed to hardly anyone else. . . . Never before had anti-radical nativism stirred the public mind so profoundly. During . . . the early months of 1920 no other kind of xenophobia even approached it in terms of vogue or impact.[20]

Nativist organizations fanned the flames of the hysteria. The New York Union League Club lobbied the state government to investigate anti-American activities by immigrants. Groups such as the National Security League and the American Defense League, founded during the war to harass German Americans, gained new legitimacy under the banner of hunting down subversive radicals. The Hollywood movie industry even jumped into the fray. Studio owners, most of them Polish or Russian immigrants, formed the Americanism Committee to use popular movies to "promote true Americanism and awaken the nation to the seriousness of the Bolshevistic threat."[21]

Many politicians were eager to score political points by criticizing immigrants. Everyone from city attorneys to the president of the United States painted newcomers as the new enemy. Commenting on this phenomenon, political satirist H.L. Mencken wrote in 1920: "The whole aim of practical politics is to keep the populace alarmed . . . by menacing it with an endless series of hobgoblins, all of them imaginary."[22]

Whether the fear of Reds was real or imaginary, a period known as the Red Scare followed. In cities throughout the nation, police raided community centers in Russian, Jewish, and other immigrant neighborhoods. People deemed suspicious were indiscriminately arrested, beaten, and jailed. In more than twenty states, laws were passed that made it a crime to express favorable opinions of communism or to join specific unions, such as the Industrial Workers of the World (IWW). Known as the Wobblies, this union was considered the most radical union in the nation.

# The Palmer Raids

On a national level, politicians and nativist organizations demanded that government agencies begin deporting radical immigrants. The attorney general of the United States, A. Mitchell Palmer, made it his mission to round up foreign-born Communists and anarchists in an action known as the Palmer Raids. These were carried out by a division of the Justice Department called the Bureau of Investigation, later known as the Federal Bureau of Investigation (FBI). The mission was led by future FBI chief J. Edgar Hoover, who assembled a list of one hundred and fifty thousand immigrants, many of them unionist or members of immigrant equality groups, suspected of sedition.

*Suspected Communist "radicals" await transport to the Deer Island immigration station in the port of Boston for examination, 1920.*

The Palmer Raids began in December 1919 when federal agents rounded up 249 well-known radical leaders, including the Lithuanian-born anarchist Emma Goldman. These immigrants were forced to leave their families behind when they were placed on a military ship, known as the *Soviet Ark,* and deported to Russia.

The Palmer Raids intensified in January 1920 when police and federal agents in thirty-three cities arrested four thousand eastern European immigrants in a single night. Officers raided social clubs, homes, bars, and pool rooms, often arresting everyone present. The detainees were handcuffed together and marched

*Lithuanian-born anarchist Emma Goldman speaks at Union Square, New York City, in 1916.*

to central processing stations. There officials attempted to separate radicals from innocent bystanders.

## "Sharp Tongues of Revolutionary Heat"

In what was the largest mass arrest in American history, ten thousand aliens were eventually rounded up and deported. Most were charged with espionage and sedition, crimes associated with promoting the success of America's enemies or espousing scurrilous beliefs about the government, flag, or armed forces.

Although the Palmer Raids were at first extremely popular, within months, public opinion turned against the attorney general when it became clear that thousands of those deported had no political affiliations but were simply arrested for belonging to immigrant social organizations. These social groups mainly provided small loans, medical insurance, language classes, and cultural activities for newcomers. By May 1920 Palmer was being openly mocked in the press because of the raids and was forced to justify his actions, writing in "The Case Against the Reds":

> Like a prairie-fire, the blaze of revolution was sweeping over every American institution of law and order . . . . It was eating its way into the homes of the American workmen, its sharp tongues of revolutionary heat were licking the altars of the churches, leaping into the belfry of the school bell, crawling into the sacred corners of American homes. . . . It is my belief that while [the Reds] have stirred discontent in our midst, while they have caused irritating strikes, and while they have infected our social ideas with the disease of their own minds and their unclean morals we can get rid of them! and not until we have done so shall we have removed the menace of Bolshevism for good. [23]

By the time Palmer's article was printed, the Red Scare was nearly over. None of the major labor strikes had achieved their goals. In an ironic twist, major corporations helped ease tensions against immigrants. The major auto, steel, rubber, mining, and shipbuilding manufacturers relied on a constant stream of foreign labor to keep wages down, and they knew that without immigrants the unionists would have a stronger hand. To ensure this did not happen, a number of famous industrialists formed a group called the Inter-Racial Council to run ads and editorials that praised immigrant workers and open immigration policies.

The final blow to the Red Scare came from Palmer himself. He predicted that anarchists and Communists would set off dozens of bombs in major cities during May Day celebrations in 1920. When no such explosions occurred, Palmer's critics vociferously mocked the attorney general in the press. Even the Supreme Court got involved, saying Palmer's illegal raids had stirred up more anti-American sentiments than the Bolsheviks and anarchists combined.

## The Rise of Anti-Semitism

Although the Red Scare was over, lingering hostility remained toward the millions of Jewish immigrants who had moved to the United States since the 1890s. The reasons were twofold. The ideology of the Bolshevik revolution was based on the *Communist Manifesto*, whose author, Karl Marx, was Jewish. In addition, several prominent revolutionaries were Jewish, including anarchist Emma Goldman and, in the Soviet Union, Leon Trotsky. While only a tiny minority of Jewish people were actual Communist Party members, bigots used these people as scapegoats to incite prejudice against all Jews.

One of the most outspoken anti-Semites of the era was also the richest and most respected man in America, Henry Ford. In May 1920 Ford began writing a series of articles that appeared on the front page of the newspaper he owned, the *Dearborn Independent*, with a circulation of seven hundred thousand. Ford contemptuously blamed Jewish people for plotting "to control the world, not by territorial acquisition, not by military aggression, not by governmental subjugation, but by control of the machinery of commerce and exchange."[24]

Ford's anti-Semitic tirades were eventually published in four volumes: *The International Jew, the World's Foremost Problem* (November 1920); *Jewish Activities in the United States* (April 1921); *Jewish Influences in American Life* (November 1921); and *Aspects of Jewish Power in the United States* (May 1922). Collectively known as *The International Jew: The World's Foremost Problem*, these books were distributed at thousands of Ford dealerships across the country and were eventually printed in dozens of languages and sold all over the world. Their destructive influence contributed to anti-Semitism abroad as well as at home: Racist arguments in the book were used by Adolf Hitler in the 1920s in developing the Nazi ideology that resulted in the Holocaust.

## The Rise of the Ku Klux Klan

Eventually, a boycott of Ford Motor Company by Jewish customers and public pressure from high-ranking politicians forced Ford to apologize for his racist columns. However, his articles about international Jewish conspiracies were echoed by a more insidious force, the Ku Klux Klan, which used racist propaganda to incite hatred of Jewish immigrants.

The Ku Klux Klan, founded by Confederate veterans after the Civil War, was revived in October 1916 by William J. Simmons in Atlanta, Georgia. The main goal of the reconstituted Klan was to terrorize African Americans through beatings, bombings, and lynchings. However, Klan leaders also railed against Jews and immigrants from Catholic countries, blaming them for diluting the purity of Anglo-Saxon culture. According to Klan Imperial Wizard Hiram Wesley Evans, writing in 1920:

> Our unity is threatened by hordes of immigrants . . . who bring foreign ideas and ideals into our land. Two things must be done: first, we must stop influx of foreigners; second, we must through education, bring all people to common program of acting and thinking.[25]

## Common Prejudices

Klan membership was restricted to white, native-born Protestants. Despite this stipulation, the Klan had little trouble signing up new members. By the mid-1920s the group reportedly had 3 to 4 million members—an estimated 15 percent of all Protestant Americans. While the stereotypical Klansman is thought of as a rural farmer from a southern state, in the 1920s Klansmen came from all walks of life. They were professionals, businesspeople, farmers, and government authorities including sheriffs, governors, and congresspersons. By 1922 the Klan was operating in forty-five states—the midwestern state of Indiana had the largest number of Klansmen per capita with up to 40 percent of the population belonging to the group.

Although the Klan is viewed today as a radical group, in the 1920s few white

*The Ku Klux Klan parades through the streets of Tulsa, Oklahoma, in 1923. In addition to terrorizing African Americans, Klan leaders also blamed Jews and immigrants from Catholic countries for, in their view, diluting the purity of Anglo-Saxon culture.*

Americans disagreed with the organization's views. During this era blacks, Jews, and immigrants were barred from most colleges, fraternal organizations, country clubs, and wealthy neighborhoods. In 1923 Mencken made this point in *Smart Set* magazine:

Not a single solitary sound reason has yet been advanced for putting the Ku Klux Klan out of business. If the Klan is against the Jews, so are half of the good hotels of the Republic and three-quarters of the good clubs. If the Klan is against the

# The Rise and Fall of the Klan

*Between 1921 and 1929 the racist vigilante group Ku Klux Klan experienced a rapid rise in popularity, followed by a stunning fall. The Anti-Defamation League Web site provides a view of the Klan in the 1920s:*

In 1915, William J. Simmons, a lifelong joiner of clubs, was inspired to . . . establish his own organization dedicated to "comprehensive Americanism.". . . The timing was perfect. The United States was struggling to meet the challenges imposed by a massive influx of immigrants, many of whom were Catholic or Jewish and few of whom spoke English. . . .

[In] the ardently xenophobic atmosphere of post–World War I America Klan membership soared. . . . By 1921, the Klan numbered almost 100,000 members and money flooded its coffers. At its peak in 1924, 40,000 uniformed Klansmen paraded through the streets of Washington, D.C., during the Democratic National Convention. . . .

As the Klan grew, so did the number and intensity of violent acts committed by its members. The group's image suffered; the hypocrisy of a self-proclaimed "law and order" organization that utilized lynchings and vigilantism did not escape public censure. . . . Scandal followed scandal and the rank-and-file became alienated by the sexual and alcoholic exploits of its leaders. By the outbreak of the Great Depression in 1929, the Klan had fragmented into dozens of independent realms and membership plummeted.

*Members of the Ku Klux Klan march down Pennsylvania Avenue in Washington, D.C., in 1925.*

"Ku Klux Klan," Anti-Defamation League, 2005. www.adl.org/learn /ext_us/KKK.asp?LEARN_Cat=Ex tremism&LEARN_SubCat=Extrem ism_in_America&x picked=4&item =kkk.

foreign-born or the hyphenated citizen, so is the National Institute of Arts and Letters. If the Klan is against the Negro, so are all of the states south of the Mason-Dixon line. If the Klan is for damnation and persecution, so is the Methodist church. If the Klan is bent upon political control, so are the American Legion and [New York politicians]. If the Klan wears grotesque uniforms, so do the Knights of Pythias and the Mystic Shriners.[26]

# Suspending Immigration

The widespread anti-immigrant sentiments expressed by the Klan and others shifted the focus of the immigrant debate. In the early years of the century, one side advocated unlimited immigration and the other advocated some restrictions such as medical, legal, and literacy tests that culled those deemed least desirable. In the early twenties, however, few argued for unlimited immigration. Instead, the debate was over how many limitations to impose.

Supporters of severe restrictions used anti-Semitism to gain political support for their point of view. In 1920 alone, about one hundred twenty thousand Jews had migrated to the United States, chased out of eastern Europe by widespread persecution that escalated at the end of World War I. Anti-Semites in the State Department issued a report saying, because of the Jewish immigration, America was being flooded with "abnormally twisted and inassimilable [Jews]—filthy, un-American, and often dangerous in their habits."[27]

The language of the State Department document was adopted by the House Committee on Immigration. Members of this committee wrote a bill in 1920 to suspend all immigration based mainly on fears of a large Jewish influx into the country.

# The Emergency Quota Act

Powerful business interests continued to reject immigration restrictions. The Senate, in response to the interests and needs of U.S. businesses, compromised. A temporary, one-year quota system was set up that limited annual immigration from each European country based on a mathematical formula. Senators analyzed the 1910 census and ascertained how many immigrants were living in the United States at that time and from which countries they had come. The new quota restricted immigration to only 3 percent of that number for each nation. In other words, if 1 million Italians were living in America in 1910, only 30,000 would be allowed to immigrate from Italy in 1921.

In practical terms, this formula cut the total number of immigrants to three hundred fifty thousand per year and favored those from the British Isles and western Europe. There was little opposition to this idea, and the Emergency Quota Act sailed through the Senate with only one opposing vote. It was signed into law by President Warren G. Harding in May 1921.

With the new restrictions in place, the State Department was put in charge of distributing a limited number of visas through U.S. embassies in foreign countries. Instead of flocking through Ellis Island, each immigrant would now be required to apply for and obtain a visa

*Polish Jews wait in quarantine in Danzig, Poland, before sailing for the United States in 1920.*

before he or she could leave home. Those who arrived without a visa would be deported.

The new restrictions of the Emergency Quota Act signaled a decisive point in American history. For the first time, strict limits were set on the numbers of people allowed into the country. The quotas also attempted to engineer the ethnic and cultural makeup of the nation, freezing the number of foreigners and Anglo-Saxons at a specific level.

## The National Origins Act

The new restrictions created chaos in America's immigration system. The complicated numerical formulas for restrictions were enforced on a month-to-month basis. After a month's quota was filled, no more immigrants would be allowed into the country until the next month. As such, the first days of every month saw dozens of steamers racing one another to find dock space in New York. Onboard the ships, thousands of immigrants fought to be the first through Ellis Island lest they be sent back. Those who did not make it were often stranded in steerage, their lives in legal limbo. Scenes of hysterically weeping people, ordered by officials back to their nations of origin, were commonplace.

Despite the problems, lawmakers believed that the quota system was a success. When the Emergency Quota Act expired after one year, it was renewed for two more. Meanwhile, Congress began work on a bill to put permanent quotas in place.

Using testimony from eugenics researchers and nativist organizations, rep-resentatives in Congress drew up a strict quota bill in 1923. It reduced annual immigration from 3 percent of the 1910 census to 2 percent of the 1890 census. Since few eastern and southern Europeans lived in the United States in 1890, this measure effectively halted all immigration from those regions.

Once again, big business opposed the bill and urged legislators not to pass it because labor shortages and economic expansion were driving wages to record levels. However, the Ku Klux Klan organized a massive letter-writing campaign to

*Once the Emergency Quota Act was enacted in 1921, shiploads of immigrants would race to be the first to arrive in New York Harbor each month so they would be admitted to the United States before the monthly quota was met.*

# "Cleansing Aliens of Foreign Customs"

*Nativist Americans had a dual strategy for dealing with immigration. They wanted to prevent foreigners from moving to the United States and they wanted to "Americanize" immigrants who were already living in the country. Robert A. Divine explains in* American Immigration Policy, 1924–1952.

[M]any people] had been concerned with the assimilation of aliens into American society . . . but gradually this concern had been taken over by more nationalistic groups, who advocated a strenuous policy of Americanization. Generally it was urged that immigration be halted for a few years until the colonies of foreign minorities had been broken up and absorbed in the social structure. The melting pot had failed to melt, charged many restrictionists, and there had to be a breathing spell during which aliens were cleansed of their foreign customs and languages and were taught American patterns of thought and speech. It is interesting to note that the majority of Americans did not view this melting pot as a process of cultural fusion by which each immigrant group contributed its share to a national mosaic. Rather it was generally believed to be a smelting process in which the immigrant was stripped of his old-world characteristics and recast in a standard American mold.

Robert A. Divine, *American Immigration Policy, 1924–1952.* New Haven, CT: Yale University Press, 1957, pp. 7–8.

Congress in support of the bill. Other anti-immigrant groups joined in and the nativist instincts of the general public prevailed. The outcome was the passage of the Immigration Act of 1924, also known as the National Origins Act.

The changes ushered in by the National Origins Act were dramatic. The law cut annual Italian immigration from 42,000 a year to 4,000. Polish immigration was cut from 31,000 to 6,000 and Greek immigration from 3,000 to 100. Meanwhile, the quotas allowed about 51,000 immigrants from Germany, 34,000 from Great Britain, and 28,000 from Ireland. In all, 86 percent of the immigrants allowed into the country every year would now come from northern Europe. Only 11 percent were from eastern and southern Europe, and about 2 percent from Africa, Australia, and the Middle East. The act also prevented all Japanese, Indian, and other Asians from moving to the United States.

While limiting immigrants from specific countries, the government also established guidelines to control the kinds of people who would be allowed even under the restrictive conditions. For example, the mothers, fathers, wives, and children of adult aliens were given priority. Only after these people were admitted could the rest of the quota be opened to applicants without family members in the United States.

The National Origins Act did not restrict immigration from Canada or Latin American countries because of the relatively small numbers of people immigrating from those regions during that time. As a result about a quarter million people continued to move to the United States throughout the 1920s. Europeans were slightly more than half that number, about a quarter were Canadians, and Latin Americans made up the rest.

## Americanizing the Immigrants

Nativist organizations celebrated the passage of the National Origins Act. With this goal accomplished, many turned to Americanizing immigrants and their offspring. Jones explains their motivation:

> Americanization of the immigrant became a patriotic duty. . . . In their anxiety to promote national unity, zealous patriots subjected immigrant groups to a high-pressure sales campaign designed to promote naturalization [citizenship],

the learning of English, and to inculcate knowledge of and respect for American institutions and ideals. . . . American nationalists began to demand a completely conformist loyalty.[28]

In the years after the passage of the National Origins Act, the white population of the United States became extremely homogenized. During the forty years that followed, the sound of foreign languages on American streets diminished. European food, arts, and entertainment became Americanized or disappeared completely. Children and grandchildren of immigrants spoke only English and deliberately ignored the traditions of their ancestors.

The grand American experiment to absorb hundreds of various cultures seemed to be over. The halls of Ellis Island no longer welcomed shiploads of huddled masses; rather, the facility became a temporary holding center for detention and deportation of aliens. Although the Statue of Liberty continued to look eastward, the majority of Americans turned their gazes inward. They were proud to celebrate their democracy and freedom, now "untainted" by foreign influence.

# Chapter Three

# Years of Isolation

In 1924 Congress had passed the most restrictive immigration bill in American history, drastically reducing the number of immigrants allowed into the United States to a few hundred thousand a year. The National Origins Act was the climax to a divisive decades-long debate over immigration issues.

After the law was passed, most Americans seemed to forget about immigration issues. This was an era known as the Roaring Twenties and the public was more interested in the soaring stock market, Prohibition and the availability of bootleg liquor, and the startling new fashions worn by women called flappers.

As the years passed, nativist groups like the Ku Klux Klan lost millions of members, their concerns no longer timely. Immigrants who had moved to United States before the restrictions became increasingly assimilated and less conspicuous. Millions of people learned English and the numbers of people speaking foreign languages fell from about 9 percent of the population in 1930 to about half that number by 1950.

Immigrants spent the years between the world wars working to become naturalized citizens. They were aided by the *Federal Textbook on Citizenship,* distributed through schools. The Immigration Service streamlined the citizenship process by creating a naturalization system. Examiners working in naturalization courts interviewed applicants and promoted uniform implementation of federal immigration policies. This process proved to be very successful. By 1940, for example, nearly 60 percent of first-generation Poles and 70 percent of Russians had become naturalized Americans.

The homogenization of American culture was doubtlessly driven by immigrants who wished to blend in with natives of their adopted country. Many remembered the deportations and anti-immigrant hysteria of the 1910s and 1920s and were fearful that such attitudes might be revived in the future.

# The Great Depression

Immigration issues were largely forgotten until October 1929, when the stock market crashed. Within a few months, it became obvious to politicians and average citizens that the United States was in for a long economic downturn later called the Great Depression.

The Great Depression also hit Canada, Europe, and economies around the world.

In this period of widespread unemployment and dire poverty, immigrants were not welcome in the United States, where one-third of the eligible workforce was unemployed. Americans once again began clamoring for even tighter immigration restrictions.

In Washington, D.C., the debate over immigration took two forms. Those who supported stringent restrictions wanted

*The 1920s was a time of excess in the United States. Women wore startling new fashions, the economy was doing well, and the "problem" of immigration was under control thanks to the National Origins Act.*

*Men gather outside a soup kitchen in 1931. Some blamed immigrants for the lack of jobs for American workers during the Great Depression.*

Congress to pass laws that would completely shut the doors to immigrants. Others with a less severe outlook favored using administrative tactics by the executive branch to limit immigration through decrees to the Immigration Service. This was an important distinction. Restrictive laws would be much harder to revoke or replace than limits implemented through the administrative process, which could easily be rescinded when economic conditions improved.

## Keeping Out the Poor

In September 1930, before Congress could pass restrictive legislation, President Herbert Hoover acted through administrative channels. In an effort to keep out all but the richest Europeans, Hoover instructed the State Department to strictly enforce the provision of the 1917 law that prohibited immigrants "likely to become a public charge."[29] This was the first time the "public charge" provision had been interpreted this way. Previously, anyone with steamship fare and a desire to find employment had been admitted into the United States.

Hoover's restrictions had the desired effect. By October 1930 only 22 percent of the quotas established by the National Origins Act were filled. By February 1931 that number was less than 10 percent. In this way, without congressional debate or new legislation, immigration was cut 90 percent in five months.

Other statistics tell an even more dramatic story. In 1924, the year the National Origins Act was passed, 630,000 Europeans moved to America. In 1929, before the Depression, that number was reduced to 210,000. After Hoover's restrictions were put into place, the number of immigrants fell to 31,000, about 5 percent of the 1924 high.

Although immigration was severely restricted by Hoover, nativist congressmen and senators continued to write legislation that would permanently bar foreigners. Nearly every year throughout the 1930s, bills were introduced that would restrict immigration to 10 percent of the 1924 quotas.

Congressman Martin Dies of Texas was a strong restrictionist who blamed immigrants for the lack of jobs during the Depression. In 1934 Dies stated: "If we had refused admission to the 16,500,000 foreign born who are living in the country today, we would have no unemployment problem to distress and harass us."[30] However, by this time the restrictionists were a minority in Congress and could not muster the support to pass new legislation.

# Rumblings of War

The Depression was only one major issue affecting American immigration policies. An even more serious problem was the rising power of Adolf Hitler in Germany. Hitler was appointed chancellor of Germany in January 1933. Within months the Third Reich government, led by Hitler and the Nazi Party, began persecuting Jews, Communists, liberals, and anyone else who opposed them. This created a wave of refugees fleeing Germany beginning with about fifty thousand Jews in 1933. In *American Immigration Policy, 1924–1952*, Robert A. Divine explains how this development began to affect American immigration policy:

This situation raised the question of whether the United States should provide a refuge for these persecuted people. The asylum ideal was an American tradition, yet one which had not been written into the immigration laws. Refugees were not distinguished from other immigrants in existing legislation except in one case—the literacy test could be waived for persons fleeing political or religious oppression. Otherwise, refugees were faced with the same barriers which obstructed the admission of all immigrants—the national origin quotas; the mental, moral, and physical tests; and the public charge clause.[31]

Throughout the rest of the decade, New York Congressman Samuel Dickstein, chairman of the Committee on Naturalization and Immigration, led efforts to ease restrictions for Jewish refugees. These measures were supported by various religious groups and many politicians. However, the entrenched anti-immigrant forces continued to oppose easing quotas for any reason. Nativist groups feared that allowing refugees to immigrate would flood the nation with Communist agitators. Labor organizations wanted to keep out foreign workers who might drive down wages. In the midst of the Depression, these arguments resonated with a majority of Americans. Meanwhile, the new president, Democrat Franklin D. Roosevelt, moved to ease the problem by ordering the State Department to process German refugees with "the most humane and favorable treatment possible under the law."[32] Roosevelt's order did little, however, to solve the problem. The Nazis continued their campaign of violent persecution against Jews whose opportunities for escape were rapidly shrinking.

## "Every Disgruntled Element"

The refugee situation became more critical in 1938 when Germany annexed Austria, creating a wave of liberal and Jewish

*In 1940, after the Nazis conquered France, the U.S. Immigration and Naturalization Service was advised to issue about thirty-two hundred visitor visas to wealthy or respected academics and professionals. Here, scientist Albert Einstein takes the United States citizenship oath in 1940.*

refugees from that nation and moving Europe closer to war. Again the president emphasized America's traditional commitment to asylum for the politically oppressed people of the world. However, opinion polls showed that more than 80 percent of the public opposed admission to refugees, fearing that such a policy would open America's doors to millions of oppressed people throughout the world. Representative John Rankin of Mississippi summed up the general view on the matter when he stated, "Almost every disgruntled element that ever got into trouble in its own country has pleaded for admission into the United States on the ground that they were oppressed at home."[33]

While restrictionists in Congress continued to resist any changes to immigration policy, Roosevelt instituted a few changes within the immigration department, now called the Immigration and Naturalization Service, or INS. Roosevelt ordered the INS to renew visitor visas every six months for fifteen thousand refugees who were already in the United States as visitors.

On September 1, 1939, Germany invaded Poland, launching World War II. The Nazis instituted a campaign to destroy Polish culture by slaughtering university professors, artists, writers, politicians, priests, and the nation's entire Jewish population. This move created a massive refugee crisis in eastern Europe but there was little change in American immigration policy. However, in 1940 after the Nazis conquered France, the INS was advised to issue about thirty-two hundred visitor visas to wealthy or respected academics and professionals. According to Roosevelt, the extra visas would go to "those of superior intellectual attainment, of indomitable spirit, experienced in vigorous support of the principles of liberal government and who are in danger of persecution or death at the hands of the autocracy."[34]

Roosevelt also changed the way visas were issued by the State Department. Previously, German refugees had to apply to the U.S. embassy in Germany to obtain a visa. Since many German citizens seeking asylum had fled to other countries, the INS was allowing embassies in Portugal, Morocco, and even China to grant visas to refugees. However, these new measures did little good. Those who were running from the Nazis were either unaware of the changes or were unable to reach a neutral port.

The failure of the visa system was most tragically illustrated by the fate of those aboard the German transatlantic liner the *St. Louis.* In 1939, with Europe on the brink of war, this ship left Hamburg for Havana, Cuba, with 937 Jewish passengers fleeing the Third Reich. The passengers were planning to obtain U.S. visas in Cuba. However, the government in Havana refused to let the ship land. The passengers were sent back to France, Holland, and Belgium. Most perished in concentration camps when the Nazis conquered those countries during the war.

## Differing Views

Despite the fate of the *St. Louis,* about 150,000 to 250,000 people were able to

# The Tragic Voyage of the *St. Louis*

*The fate of the Jewish refugees aboard the German ship* St. Louis *is described on "The Holocaust Chronicle" Web site:*

The tragic story of the journey of the German ocean liner *St. Louis* epitomized the desperate and futile struggle of Jews trying to escape Germany.

On May 15, 1939, the Nazis allowed more than 900 Jews on the liner, which set sail for Cuba. Hopeful passengers carried what they believed were valid permits guaranteeing them temporary stay until visas and permanent refuge in the United States could be secured. Shockingly, on arrival at Havana, Cuba, only 29 were allowed to disembark. The rest were refused entry under revised Cuban immigration restrictions. When the ship was ordered to leave the harbor, several passengers attempted suicide. Cuban police boats shadowed the *St. Louis* in case passengers tried to jump ship.

For three days the liner cruised slowly off the U.S. coast, waiting in vain for America to accept its human cargo. In mid-June, after 35 days of aimless sailing, the *St. Louis* was forced to return to Europe, where the governments of England, France, Holland, and Belgium finally agreed to divide the passengers between them. The world's press followed the ship's sad journey, even recording it on newsreels.

"1939: The War Against The Jews," *The Holocaust Chronicle*, 2002. www.holocaustchronicle.org/Static Pages/161.html.

*German Jewish refugees crowd the deck of the S.S.* St. Louis *in 1939.*

emigrate from Germany and Austria to the United States in the late 1930s. The majority of these people were Jewish and they entered the country through the established quota system, which allowed about 51,000 each year from Germany and about half that many from Austria. During that period, the U.S. took in more refugees than any other country. Describing this situation, Divine writes:

> Thus even though Roosevelt's attempts to solve the refugee problem on an international level failed, he was able to thwart the restrictionist majority in Congress and maintain to a very large degree the American ideal of asylum for the oppressed of Europe. Considering that throughout this period the United States was engulfed in the worst depression in history, the relief given to refugees was a major humanitarian achievement.[35]

Others disagree with Divine's analysis, believing that Roosevelt, who was very popular among American Jews, could have done more to help those who were desperate to leave Europe. Discussing the issue, Roger Daniels writes in *Coming to America*, "The adherence to the status quo by our most innovative president led to one of the major moral blots on the American public record: our essential indifference to the fate of Jewish and other refugees from Hitler's Third Reich."[36]

The refugee issue was dwarfed by news of the conflict after World War II began in Europe in 1939. However, the American government, in preparation for U.S. involvement in the war, instituted a series of changes within the INS. In 1940 jurisdiction of the service was moved from the State Department to the Justice Department. This was done because of the growing perception that immigration was no longer an economic matter but a national security issue. Within the Justice Department, the FBI was put in charge of checking the visas of those who might have close ties to the German or Austrian governments. The policy change was due to the widespread belief that Nazi spies and saboteurs might try to enter the United States disguised as refugees. In coordination with the changes, the INS instituted the Alien Registration Program to record the names and fingerprints of every immigrant in the United States.

## Enemy Aliens

In December 1941 the United States entered World War II allied with Great Britain and the Soviet Union, declaring war on Japan, Germany, and Italy, collectively known as the Axis Powers. With the nation at war, immigration basically came to a halt. Meanwhile, immigrants of German, Austrian, and Italian heritage who were already in the United States were facing increased scrutiny and suspicion. In late December 1941 about sixteen thousand recent immigrants living near defense installations and factories were rounded up and questioned by local authorities and the FBI. Most were released within a few weeks. However, the INS required them, as well as all those born in Japan, to register with the government as "enemy aliens." By October 1942 the enemy alien status was lifted for Italians and most Germans because they were not perceived as a threat.

Japanese Americans were treated much differently than the Europeans. Japan had bombed the U.S. naval base at Pearl Harbor, Hawaii, on December 7, 1941. The surprise attack on the American fleet killed more than twenty-four hundred military personnel and was the direct cause of the U.S. decision to enter the war. After the attack, there was a widespread, if irrational, belief that a Japanese invasion of the West Coast was imminent.

At the time, there were about one hundred twenty thousand people of Japanese ancestry living on the West Coast. Two-thirds of these of people were Americans, having been born in the United States. Some were even military veterans from World War I. The other third were born in Japan. Although many would have preferred to become naturalized, they were barred from ever becoming citizens by laws passed earlier in the century.

Whether or not they were citizens, the Japanese were caught between two nations at war, as Thomas Archdeacon writes in *Becoming American: An Ethnic History:* "Despite the Constitution's guarantee of citizenship to all natives of the United States, many people refused to accord to Japanese-Americans the same protections and presumptions of loyalty that they gave Germans and Italians of second or later generations."[37]

## Executive Order 9066

Negative racial stereotypes about Japanese people were prominently expressed in newspapers, by powerful politicians, and by a large majority of the American public. In Washington, D.C., military leaders argued that national security was more important than constitutional guarantees of civil rights as far as they applied to Japanese Americans. National security was not the only motive: Citizens on the West Coast were eager to take over the farmlands and businesses owned by Japanese people. This point was emphasized by Attorney General Francis Biddle in February 1942:

> For several weeks there have been increasing demands for evacuation of all Japanese, aliens and citizens alike, from the West Coast states. A great many West Coast people distrust the Japanese, various special interests would welcome their removal from good farm land and the elimination of their competition. . . . My last advice from the War Department is that there is no evidence of imminent attack and from the F.B.I. that there is no evidence of planned sabotage.[38]

Despite the assessments by the attorney general and the FBI, in February 1942 Roosevelt issued Executive Order 9066, revoking the rights of Japanese immigrants and Japanese Americans. The order authorized the secretary of war and military commanders to arrest and relocate any persons deemed a threat to the United States. Although Executive Order 9066 could have been used against anybody, it was applied solely to about forty thousand Japanese nationals (called Issei)

# UNITED STATES DEPARTMENT OF JUSTICE

★

# NOTICE
# TO ALIENS OF ENEMY
# NATIONALITIES

★ The United States Government requires all aliens of German, Italian, or Japanese nationality to apply at post offices nearest to their place of residence for a Certificate of Identification. Applications must be filed between the period February 9 through February 28, 1942. *Go to your postmaster today for printed directions.*

FRANCIS BIDDLE,
*Attorney General.*

EARL G. HARRISON,
*Special Assistant to the Attorney General.*

## AVVISO

Il Governo degli Stati Uniti ordina a tutti gli stranieri di nazionalità Tedesca, Italiana e Giapponese di fare richiesta all' Ufficio Postale più prossimo al loro luogo di residenza per ottenere un Certificato d'Identità. Le richieste devono essere fatte entro il periodo che decorre tra il 9 Febbraio e il 28 Febbraio, 1942.

*Andate oggi dal vostro Capo d'Ufficio Postale (Postmaster) per ricevere le istruzioni scritte.*

## BEKANNTMACHUNG

Die Regierung der Vereinigten Staaten von Amerika fordert alle Auslaender deutscher, italienischer und japanischer Staatsangehoerigkeit auf, sich auf das ihrem Wohnorte naheliegende Postamt zu begeben, um einen Personalausweis zu beantragen. Das Gesuch muss zwischen dem 9. und 28. Februar 1942 eingereicht werden.

*Gehen Sie noch heute zu Ihrem Postmeister und verschaffen Sie sich die gedruckten Vorschriften.*

敵國外人注意

日獨伊諸國ノ國籍ヲ有スル在留外人ハ
二月九日ヨリ二十八日マデノ間ニ其共居所ニ一番
近イ郵便局デ自分證明書ヲ申込ム可シ。
含モ早速郵便局ヘ行キテ説明書ヲ賴ム樣ニ願ヒマ大。

**Post This Side In All States EXCEPT**
**Arizona, California, Idaho, Montana, Nevada, Oregon, Utah, Washington**

*In December 1941 the United States entered World War II, declaring war on Japan. Immigrants from these nations were required to register with the government as "enemy aliens."*

*In 1942 Japanese immigrants and Japanese Americans in the western United States were forced from their homes into relocation camps by Executive Order 9066. Pictured here is the relocation camp at Santa Anita, California.*

and eighty thousand Japanese Americans (called Nisei) who lived in Alaska, southern Arizona, and along the West Coast.

The roundup began in May when notices were posted in Japanese neighborhoods in Los Angeles, San Francisco, and elsewhere. Both alien and non-alien Japanese were told to assemble at particular points and bring with them bedding and linens, toilet articles, eating utensils, and extra clothing for each member of the family. Pets were not permitted. Among the prisoners were thousands of women,

children, and senior citizens. Despite their compliance with government dictates, they were held behind barbed wire and under armed guard.

While the government built permanent concentration camps in remote desert areas, the Japanese were taken to twelve temporary detention centers. After about seven months they were transported to ten internment camps hastily constructed on Native American reservations in places such as Gila Bend, Arizona; Granada, Colorado; Minidoka,

Idaho; and Manzanar, California. Each camp held about ten thousand people. The bleak camps consisted of tar paper barracks that provided little protection from the sweltering 100°F (37.8°C) summer days and frigid winter nights where temperatures fell below zero.

## Proving Their Loyalty

After being interned, the government asked the Japanese prisoners to pledge their loyalty to the United States. About 90 percent gladly affirmed their allegiance. Those who did not, most of them aliens, feared that by doing so they would lose their Japanese citizenship and become stateless.

The best way for many men to leave the camps was to join the U.S. army and in 1943, about thirty-three thousand did so. They served as combat soldiers, intelligence agents, and interpreters. Many were assigned to the segregated 442nd Regimental Combat Team serving in Europe. Although their family members were imprisoned in internment camps,

# Assessing the Loyalty of Japanese Americans

*In the months before the Japanese attack on Pearl Harbor, Special Representative of the State Department Curtis B. Munson carried out an intelligence-gathering investigation on the loyalty of Japanese Americans, or Nisei. The report is excerpted below:*

Second generation [Nisei] who have received their whole education in the United States and usually, in spite of discrimination against them and a certain amount of insults accumulated through the years from irresponsible elements, show . . .[an] eagerness to be Americans. . . .

There are still Japanese in the United States who will tie dynamite around their waist and make a human bomb out of themselves. We grant this, but today they are few. . . . [The Nisei] are universally estimated from 90 to 98 percent loyal to the United States. . . . They are not Japanese in culture. They are foreigners to Japan. Though American citizens they are not accepted by Americans, largely because they look differently and can be easily recognized. . . . The loyal Nisei hardly knows where to turn. Some gesture of protection or wholehearted acceptance of this group would go a long way to swinging them away from any last romantic hankering after old Japan. They are not oriental or mysterious, they are very American and are of a proud, self-respecting race suffering from a little inferiority complex.

Curtis B. Munson, "The Munson Report," *The Japanese-American Internment*, April 15, 1996. www.geo cities.com/Athens/8420/generations.html.

soldiers of the 442nd fought honorably and became the most decorated combat unit of its size in the entire U.S. military. Together they won over 18,000 decorations including 7 Presidential Distinguished Unit Citations, a Congressional Medal of Honor, 47 Distinguished Service Crosses, 350 Silver Stars, 810 Bronze Stars, and more than 3,600 Purple Hearts.

On January 2, 1945, just months before the end of the war when U.S. victory was all but assured, the president rescinded Executive Order 9066. Tens of thousands of Japanese returned home to find that their houses, lands, and businesses had been taken over by others. While most simply tried to resume their lives, others fought to regain what they had lost. It was not until 1988, however, that Congress passed a bill apologizing to the Japanese for the injustices they had suffered during the wartime hysteria. About sixty thousand surviving former prisoners were granted twenty thousand dollars each as compensation for their losses, but the money was not made available until 1993.

## The Bracero Program

In the last years of the war, hundreds of Japanese were allowed to leave the internment camps to work as agricultural laborers. The war had caused a severe labor shortage and these people were needed to pick crops. To further alleviate the labor problem, politically powerful ranchers and farmers in California lobbied the INS to set up a program to import farm hands from Mexico. The result was the bracero program. In *Inside the State* Kitty Calavita explains the name of the program:

The term "bracero" comes from the Spanish word for arm, "brazos," and can be translated loosely in this context as "farmhand." Its literal meaning "arm-man," hints at the function these braceros were to play in the agricultural economy, supplying a pair of arms and imposing few obligations on the host society as human beings.[39]

Whatever the implications of the name, the bracero program was unusual in that it was quietly launched without any public discussion or congressional debate. It was simply set up by an informal agreement between Mexico and the United States. The Mexican government acted as a representative of the workers while the U.S. government represented the farm employers. The agreement established that braceros would be paid a minimum wage of 30 cents an hour, equal to about $3.70 an hour today. In addition, farmers contracting the workers would pay the INS for their transportation to and from Mexico.

The bracero program began on September 29, 1942, when five hundred Mexican farmhands were bused to private farms in Stockton, California. The workers were experienced agricultural laborers who picked sugar beets by day and lived in barracks at night. From these modest beginnings, the bracero program grew into the largest foreign worker program in U.S. history. By 1945 about two hundred fifteen thousand Mexican nationals had been employed under the program.

Although braceros were employed in at least twenty-four states, the large majority worked in California and Texas,

*A border patrol officer checks the identification of a legal Mexican worker in El Centro, California. The bracero program, started in 1942, allowed Mexican workers who were not citizens to work legally in the United States as farmhands.*

picking cotton, beets and other vegetables, and fruit. They were seldom treated fairly and growers often found ways to bypass the conditions of the program. As such, the minimum wage was rarely paid, hours were long and grueling, and humane standards for housing and feeding the workers were often ignored.

When the war ended, returning Ame can farmworkers found that they had bee replaced by braceros. Demands were made to end the program but growers petitioned their representatives in Congress to keep it in place. Using an argument that is echoed today, the farm contractors argued that Americans were unwilling to do the "stoop

*Mexicans cross the Rio Grande in search of farm jobs in the United States in 1948. Between 1947 and 1949, 74,600 braceros legally worked within the program while nearly twice as many undocumented workers worked beside them in the fields.*

work" of agriculture. Therefore the bracero program was crucial for keeping food prices low and the farm economy healthy. The government agreed and the bracero program was kept in place until 1964.

## Illegal Immigrants

Because braceros provided an endless supply of cheap labor, both the government and growers considered the program to be an ideal system. This attitude was seen in a 1951 report published by the President's Commission on Migratory Labor:

> [Growers] want a labor supply which, on one hand, is ready and willing to meet the short-term work requirements and which, on the other hand, will not impose social and economic problems on them or on their community when the work is finished. . . . The demand for migratory workers is thus essentially twofold: To be ready to go to work when needed; to be gone when not needed.[40]

Despite the statements in the report, many braceros did not leave when the work ended. Instead, they stayed illegally in the United States, where they married and raised families.

The bracero program contributed to illegal immigration in other ways. For example, thousands who wished to join the program congregated on the United States–Mexico border, which was not heavily patrolled as it is today. Those who were not accepted by the program simply walked or drove into the United States, where they found work on their own.

By the late 1940s illegal immigration began to soar along the southern border, prompted in part by the government's lax oversight of the bracero program. The President's Commission on Migratory Labor report admitted this failure: "Following the war . . . we virtually abandoned effective scrutiny and enforcement of [the Bracero Program] to which private employers and Mexican aliens were parties."[41]

## "Drying Out the Wetbacks"

In the post–World War II years, many workers began to ignore the bracero program completely. Between 1947 and 1949, 74,600 braceros legally worked within the program while nearly twice as many undocumented workers worked beside them in the fields. In 1950 the numbers were more startling. Twenty thousand braceros were imported to work; 96,000 illegal aliens worked beside them. To deal with the situation, the INS simply legalized, or "paroled," any workers already in the United States. In a common derogatory reference, Mexicans were officially referred to as wetbacks and within the INS, the process of paroling the illegal immigrants was known as "drying out"[42] the wetbacks. When news of the drying-out policy got back to Mexico, it encouraged even more people to illegally immigrate to the United States.

Illegal immigration was also aided by the policies of the U.S. Border Patrol, created in 1924 to police the border. During the 1940s and 1950s the Border Patrol refused to pick up and deport illegal immigrants during peak agricultural seasons

# Operation Wetback

*In 1954 political pressure forced the Border Patrol to round up and deport thousands of undocumented Mexican farmworkers in California, Arizona, and Texas. The sweep known as Operation Wetback is described below by social sciences professor Fred L. Koestler:*

Operation Wetback, a national reaction against illegal immigration, began in Texas in mid-July 1954. . . . [The] United States Border Patrol aided by municipal, county, state, and federal authorities, as well as the military, began a quasi-military operation of search and seizure of all illegal immigrants. . . . On July 15, the first day of the operation, 4,800 aliens were apprehended. Thereafter the daily totals dwindled to an average of about 1,100 a day. The forces used by the government were actually relatively small, perhaps no more than 700 men, but were exaggerated by border patrol officials who hoped to scare illegal workers into flight back to Mexico. . . . It is difficult to estimate the number of illegal aliens forced to leave by the operation. The INS claimed as many as 1,300,000, though the number officially apprehended did not come anywhere near this total. The INS estimate rested on the claim that most aliens, fearing apprehension by the government, had voluntarily repatriated themselves before and during the operation. . . .Critics of Operation Wetback considered it xenophobic and heartless.

Fred L. Koestler, "Operation Wetback," *The Handbook of Texas Online*, June 6, 2001. www.tsha.utexas. edu/handbook/online/articles/OO/pqo1.html.

in the spring and fall. As Willard Kelly, chief of the Border Patrol, stated in 1950: "Service Officers were instructed to defer the apprehensions of Mexicans employed on Texas farms where to remove them would likely result in the loss of the crops."[43] These orders often came from powerful political sources. For example, Allan Shivers, governor of Texas from 1949 to 1957, was the largest employer of illegal immigrants in the state and the Border Patrol was instructed to stay away from his ranch during harvest season. However, in the off seasons the Border Patrol was known to make highly publicized sweeps and round up thousands of undocumented immigrants for deportation. The most well known was "Operation Wetback," conducted in 1954.

## A Policy Paradox

The bracero program and the illegal immigration it encouraged illustrates the paradox in U.S. immigration policy during the 1940s and early 1950s. While zealously denying admission to European refugees and immigrants, at least a million Mexicans were illegally allowed into the country as the INS looked the other way. This policy, driven by monetary rather than humanitarian concerns, remained in place for decades. While Europeans and Japanese were shut out of the United States by strict immigration policies, Mexican farmhands and their families slowly changed the face of American culture in the Southwest.

# Chapter Four

# Opening the Doors

Between the 1920s and the end of World War II, immigration policies in the United States were based on stringent quotas and restrictions spelled out in the National Origins Act. While millions of people wanted to immigrate to America, only a small percentage were allowed to do so. However, the events of the war and its aftermath prompted several policy reversals that would have far-reaching effects.

At first the changes were very minor. In the 1950s, however, they began to take on a greater importance as new groups of people were allowed into the United States. Many of these people were admitted under a new legal classification, that of refugee. This was a major reversal of the policy that prevented refugees fleeing fascist regimes in World War II from migrating to the United States. .

After the refugee policies chipped away at quota restrictions, they were nearly abolished in 1965, thirty-six years after

they were put into place. This ushered in a new era of American multiculturalism that could be compared to the first decades of the early 1900s.

## Chinese Inclusion

The first changes in policy were minor. But they were aimed squarely at the first immigration law ever written in the United States, the Chinese Exclusion Act of 1882. More than sixty years after its passage, the law was repealed during World War II, when China and the United States were allied against the Japanese. Because of the brutal Japanese occupation of China, many Americans became sympathetic toward the Chinese. In the spirit of the times, Washington senator Warren G. Magnuson proposed the Chinese Exclusion Repeal Act, which was signed into law in December 1943. This bill had a limited effect, however, since it was based on a quota system similar to the one that restricted European immigration. Under the

Chinese Exclusion Repeal Act, immigration would be limited to a number equal to one-sixth of 1 percent of the Chinese in America in 1920. This amounted to only 105 people a year.

## The Postwar Debate

When World War II ended, Chinese immigration quotas remained tight for many years. However, the prewar policies toward European immigration were called into question after the horrors of the Holocaust were revealed to the public for the first time. Between 1941 and 1945 the Nazis had rounded up and killed at least 6 million Jews along with millions of others who opposed their regime. However, in the years before this mass murder began, Hitler offered to allow about 2 million German and Austrian Jews to immigrate to the United States, Canada, and elsewhere. In the United States his offer was refused because of America's tight immigration quotas, enacted in 1924. Hitler disparaged this policy in September 1938:

> [Americans] complain . . . of the boundless cruelty with which Germany— and now Italy also—seek to rid themselves of their Jewish elements. All these great democratic empires taken together have only a handful of people to the square kilometer. Both in Italy and Germany there are over 140. Yet formerly Germany, without blinking an eyelid, for whole decades admitted these Jews by the hundred thousand. But now . . . these countries with icy coldness assured us that obviously there was no place for the Jews in their territory. . . . So no help is given.[44]

After the war, when it became obvious that millions of Jews could have been saved if the INS would have let them immigrate to the United States, the quotas were closely examined. As Daniels explains, "The memory of what the United States had done—and failed to do—about refugees in the pre-war period was an important part of the debate that raged in the late 1940s and early 1950s."[45]

*A group of World War II displaced persons (DPs) attempts to find a new home in war-torn Europe. The Displaced Persons Act of 1948 allowed about one hundred thousand DPs to immigrate to the United States annually over and above the quota numbers in the National Origins Act.*

## Displaced Persons

In the postwar era immigration concerns centered on about 10 million European refugees who had been uprooted from their now-destroyed homes and had nowhere to go. These people were referred to as "displaced persons" or, more commonly, DPs. The United States was not willing to allow all of Europe's DPs to immigrate, and the matter was a subject of heated deliberations in Congress. However, after two years of wrestling with the problem, Congress passed the Displaced Persons Act of 1948. The law allowed about one hundred thousand DPs to immigrate annually over and above the quota numbers in the National Origins Act.

The people covered by the Displaced Persons Act came from a wide range of circumstances, including a few thousand Jews who had survived the Holocaust. However, as in early years, the law continued to favor northern Europeans. According to sociologist Nathan Glazer in *Clamor at the Gates*, "The bill, unbelievably, discriminated against the Jewish survivors of the war and in favor of the ethnic Germans who had been expelled from Soviet Russia and the Baltic States."[46]

Whatever the background of the DPs, the Displaced Persons Act was the first

# Refugees and Displaced Persons

*When Congress passed the Displaced Persons Act of 1948, the bill defined refugees and DPs using a description written into the Constitution of the United Nations International Refugee Organization (IRO):*

[A] person who has left, or who is outside of, his country of nationality or of former habitual residence, and who, whether or not he had retained his nationality, belongs to one of the following categories: victims of the nazi or fascist régimes or of régimes which took part on their side in the second world war. . . . [Persons] who were considered refugees before the outbreak of the second world war, for reasons of race, religion, nationality or political opinion. . . . [The] term "refugee" also applies to persons who, having resided in Germany or Austria, and being of Jewish origin or foreigners or stateless persons, were victims of nazi persecution and were detained in, or were obliged to flee from, and were subsequently returned to, one of those countries as a result of enemy action, or of war circumstances, and have not yet been firmly resettled *therein.*

*"Constitution of the International Refugee Organization," Australian Treaty Series, 2005. www.austlii.edu. au/au/other/dfat/treaties/1948/16.html.*

piece of legislation ever written that defined a refugee policy that superseded immigration policy. Under this law, about 450,000 DPs were admitted to the United States between 1948 and 1952 when the law expired. During these years another 325,000 were admitted annually under the old quota system.

## Minor Changes

In the early 1950s, for the first time in nearly thirty years, public opinion turned in favor of relaxing immigration standards. According to Robert A. Divine, "The spirit of international cooperation which pervaded the country during the war and immediately afterward led many to believe that the time had arrived for the liberalization of the immigration laws."[47]

At the same time, the Cold War had begun between the United States and the Soviet Union, its World War II ally and now superpower rival. Many Americans were still fearful that the Soviets planned to force communism on weaker nations throughout the world, and might even invade the United States. Amid mutual antagonism, both superpower nations began a massive military buildup. Cold War policies also affected the immigration debate, with both sides referring to the Soviet Union when making their arguments for or against restrictions. For example, anti-restrictionists opposed the quota system because it allowed Soviet propagandists to label Americans as racists for barring Japanese, Korean, Caribbean, Indian, and other non-Caucasian immigrants. However, restrictionists believed that open immigration would allow So-

viet agents to infiltrate American society. As Nevada senator Patrick McCarran, a staunch anti-Communist, stated, "If we destroy the internal security of this country by opening the floodgates of unlimited immigration . . .we have destroyed the national security of the United States."[48]

McCarran, the son of Irish immigrants, was chairman of the Senate Judiciary Committee and was in a powerful position to limit immigration. In 1950 McCarran produced a complex immigration bill, cosponsored by Pennsylvania representative Francis Walters, that advocated retaining the national origins system but opening the doors to small numbers of people from other nations. Although this was seen as a minor change, immigration opponents fought to defeat the bill for two years.

## The McCarran-Walters Act

By the time Congress passed the Immigration and Nationality Act (INA) of 1952, also known as the McCarran-Walters Act, the law made slight changes concerning immigration policies. Now quotas were extended to all countries, not just those in Europe, and people from Japan, Korea, and other Asian nations could apply to immigrate to the United States. This provision was seen as largely symbolic, however, since it restricted immigration to only one hundred people a year from Asian countries.

The INA retained 70 percent of all quotas for natives of just three northern European countries—the United Kingdom, Ireland, and Germany. These went mostly unused because people in those countries were not eager to move to the United States at that time. However, the unused quotas could not be assigned to people of other nations. Commenting on this inequity, President Harry Truman stated:

> The idea behind this discriminatory policy, to put it boldly, was that Americans with English or Irish names were better people and better citizens than Americans with Italian, Greek, or Polish names. . . . Such a concept is entirely unworthy of our traditions and ideals.[49]

ous, disloyal, or subversive. This provision could be used to bar members of the Communist Party. However, in most nations ruled by the Soviet Union, such membership was mandatory for professionals, even if they did not support the Communist system.

The McCarran-Walters Act was opposed by many groups that saw it as a continuation of the National Origins Act. Truman thought that the act was un-American and vetoed it, saying "it discriminated deliberately and intentionally against many of the peoples of the world."[50] However, Congress overrode

The McCarran-Walters Act prevented immigration in other ways. Under the quota system, preferences were given to immigrants with special skills—50 percent of a country's quota was reserved for highly skilled workers, scientists, researchers, professionals, and professors. Another 20 percent was set aside for the spouses and unmarried adult children of permanent resident aliens. Non-preference applicants were then allowed to fill out the remaining 30 percent of each national quota.

The McCarran-Walters Act also contained a controversial provision addressing Cold War concerns, allowing the exclusion and deportation of anyone considered danger-

*Senator Pat McCarran, one of the authors of the Immigration and Nationality Act of 1952, worried that unlimited immigration would undermine the internal security of the United States.*

Truman's veto and the McCarran-Walters Act became law. In defending his bill McCarran stated:

> [We] have in the United States today hard-core, indigestible blocs which have not become integrated into the American way of life, but which, on the contrary are its deadly enemies. Today, as never before, untold millions are storming our gates for admission and those gates are cracking under the strain. The solution of the problems of Europe and Asia will not come through a transplanting of those problems en masse to the United States.[51]

## "Whom Shall We Welcome"

After the McCarran-Walters Act was passed Truman retaliated by forming his own commission to study the quota system, the Committee on Immigration and Naturalization. In early 1953 the committee issued the report "Whom Shall We Welcome," which condemned the McCarran-Walters Act and recommended several major changes that would liberalize and modernize U.S. immigration law.

The report called for eliminating the quota system in favor of distributing a specific number of visas to applicants without regard to their national origin, race, or religious beliefs. Assignment priorities would be based on several factors including the right of asylum for refugees and DPs, family reunification, the need for skilled workers, and general immigration requests. The maximum number of people allowed to immigrate every year would be set at 251,162—less than 1.5 percent of the population in 1950. This number would be adjusted every ten years after the new census was taken.

By the time the report was released, Truman was out of office and a more conservative president, Republican Dwight D. Eisenhower, was sworn in. Eisenhower ignored the recommendations in "Whom Shall We Welcome" while McCarran falsely claimed the report was inspired by Communists working within the federal government.

## The Refugee Relief Act

While "Whom Shall We Welcome" would be shelved until the 1960s, Eisenhower was devising other means to open America's doors to immigrants. At the time, thousands of refugees were fleeing Communist East Germany and Eastern Europe. By allowing these people to immigrate, the United States would score an important propaganda victory over the Soviet Union by embracing those uprooted by communism. Motivated by this opportunity, Congress passed the Refugee Relief Act of 1953, allowing two hundred five thousand immigrants above the quota numbers established by the McCarran-Walters Act. When signing the bill, Eisenhower stated that it was a "stirring example of . . . statesmanship [that] demonstrates again America's traditional concern for the homeless, the persecuted and the less fortunate of other lands."[52]

The Refugee Relief Act admitted only those fleeing Communist regimes, mainly Germans fleeing East Germany. However,

*President Dwight D. Eisenhower signed the Refugee Relief Act of 1953, which initially admitted only those fleeing Communist regimes.*

it also included five thousand visas annually for Asians fleeing Communist China.

Once the Refugee Relief Act was in place, it was amended several times to deal with crises in various parts of the world. In 1957 the law was expanded to include people fleeing Communist oppression in Hungary, the Middle East, and North Africa. In 1960 the act was rewritten once again to include Cubans fleeing Fidel Castro's regime.

## Petitioning Congress

The Refugee Relief Act was not the only way to get around the McCarran-Walters quotas. Those who were not running from communism had another method for gaining admission to the United States. Their American relatives could petition members of Congress for entry visas. With no restrictions on this method for obtaining entry visas, by the early 1960s about three thousand five hundred such petitions were introduced annually, amounting to half the bills introduced to Congress.

One example of a petition concerned an Italian immigrant with three small children whose wife was barred from immi-

grating to America because she had been convicted of an offense in Italy. Her crime was stealing bundles of sticks to heat her home in 1913. She was denied admission to the United States until an official act of Congress allowed her to immigrate.

## "Those with the Greatest Ability"

The inflexibility of the McCarran-Walters Act meant that millions of people were finding loopholes to avoid its restrictions. This meant that two-thirds of the 5 million immigrants who came to America after

# Operation Paperclip

*Besides refugees and displaced persons, another class of Germans was allowed to immigrate above and beyond the quota system after World War II. Under a program of strict secrecy called Operation Paperclip, the Department of Defense and the Central Intelligence Agency imported about sixteen hundred German scientists, intelligence officers, and their families, most of whom had been ardent supporters of the Nazis. According to the Web article "Operation Paperclip":*

Many had been longtime members of the Nazi party and the Gestapo, had conducted experiments on humans at concentration camps, had used slave labor, and had committed other war crimes. The best-known example is Wernher von Braun. Though suspected of having used slave labor and having received honors from [the Nazis] for excellent service to the war effort, he became the father of American rocketry [and the chief scientist overseeing the U.S. space program].

"Operation Paperclip," *The Truth Seeker,* June 29, 2006. www.thetruth seeker.co.uk/article.asp?ID=122.

*Wernher von Braun in 1955.*

World War II came as entrants outside the quota system. Increasingly, politicians searched for a new immigration system to replace the old, ineffective one.

After John F. Kennedy was elected president in 1960, he expressed strong opposition to the quota system, calling it "arbitrary and unjust."[53] Making his point in a July, 1963 speech about immigration, Kennedy explained that under the act, the tiny nation of Andorra, with 6,500 people, had an immigration quota of 100 while neighboring Spain, with 30 million people, had a quota of 250. Meanwhile, immigration was limited to 100 people annually from Pakistan, Japan, Australia, and New Zealand.

Kennedy proposed amending the McCarran-Walters Act. He wanted to continue favoring skilled workers and relatives of U.S. citizens but do away with any quota system. According to Kennedy:

It should be modified so that those with the greatest ability to add to the national welfare, no matter where they are born, are granted the highest priority. The next priority should go to those who seek to be reunited with relatives. For applicants with equal claims, the earliest registrant should be first admitted.[54]

As in earlier times, plans to loosen immigration quotas were opposed by staunch anti-Communists on national security grounds. Testifying during 1964 immigration hearings before Congress, Marion Moncure Duncan, head of the patriotic society Daughters of the American Revolution, summed up the fears of many:

Since it is a recognized fact that free migration allowing unhampered movement of [enemy] agents is necessary for [the] triumph . . . of international communism as a world conspiracy, this would explain the motivation on the part of enemies of this country for concentrated effort to undermine the existing immigration law.[55]

## "Basically Immoral and Wrong"

Duncan was not alone in this belief. A 1965 poll showed that 58 percent of Americans strongly opposed easing immigration restrictions. However, the early 1960s was a time of profound social change in the United States. For example, widespread civil rights protests in the South had drawn national attention to segregation and lack of voting rights suffered by African Americans. In response to the civil rights movement, Congress passed two landmark pieces of legislation, the Civil Rights Act of 1964 and the Voting Rights Act of 1965. These bills, guaranteeing basic rights to millions of African Americans, have long been hailed as turning points for bringing equality and justice to American society. However, another law passed at the time, the Immigration and Naturalization Services Act of 1965, also known as the INS Act, was largely overlooked. As Otis L. Graham Jr. writes in *Unguarded Gates*, immigration reform was "a minor issue to the public, not on the radar screen in a decade overheated with social movements."[56]

Despite a lack of public attention, the INS Act was a major piece of legislation inspired by the Civil Rights and Voting Rights acts. Glazer explains:

> The attempt to freeze the composition of the American people by favoring Northwestern Europe was increasingly seen as basically immoral and wrong. Thus in the atmosphere of 1964 and 1965, when America's unfinished business in regard to race, poverty, and prejudice was attacked with determination, immigration was not left out.[57]

The Immigration Act of 1965 raised the annual ceiling on immigration from 150,000 to 290,000 people per year. It allo-cated 170,000 visas to people in countries in the Eastern Hemisphere and 120,000 to people in the Western Hemisphere. Each Eastern Hemisphere country was allowed an allotment of no more than 20,000 visas, while in the Western Hemisphere there was no limit per country. Non-quota immigrants, such as refugees and immediate relatives of U.S. citizens, were not counted in calculating the ceilings.

## The Aftermath

The INS Act was passed overwhelmingly by Congress—the House voted 326 to 69 in favor of the act while the Senate voted 76 to 18. President Lyndon B. Johnson signed the bill into law on October 3, 1965,

*President Lyndon B. Johnson signs the Immigration and Naturalization Services Act of 1965, which raised the annual ceiling on immigration from 150,000 to 290,000 people per year.*

beneath the Statue of Liberty. It was a striking scene, as dignitaries at the event could see the dilapidated and abandoned immigration buildings on Ellis Island in the distance. Perhaps more remarkable were Johnson's words, as he tried to reassure Americans that the new law posed no threat to their way of life: "This bill that we sign today is not a revolutionary bill. It does not affect the lives of millions. It will not reshape the structure of our daily lives, or really add importantly to our wealth and power. "[58]

But Johnson could not have been more mistaken. The INS Act opened America's doors to millions of people and reshaped the country. Despite the ceiling of 290,000 spelled out in the bill, the number of family reunification visas was unlimited and in the years following the law's enactment, from 300,000 to 800,000 immigrants moved to America. And while Johnson supported the INS Act to "redress the wrong done to those from southern or eastern Europe,"[59] legal immigration from Europe dwindled after 1965. By the late 1970s only about 65,000 people moved to America from European nations, about half as many as in 1965. However, during those years, immigration from Latin America increased over 30 percent while Asian immigration surged by nearly 40 percent.

In the fifteen years after the INS Act went into effect, over 7 million new immigrants moved to the United States. Proponents of the act point out that this may sound like a high number, but the nation's population had grown as a whole, and new immigrants accounted for only about 2 percent of the nation's population annually. This is compared to 4 to 10 percent during the first decades of the twentieth century. In addition, with favor given to those from professional and technical backgrounds, the new immigrants were, on average, better educated than those in the past.

## A New Influx of Refugees

One problem critics found with the INS Act is that it set aside only 7,400 visas annually for non-European refugees. However, during the second half of the 1960s, about 100,000 anti-Castro Cubans were moving to the United States every year. These people could not meet the technical requirements for a visa but were allowed to enter the country for humanitarian purposes, or "paroled," in the words of the government.

In the mid-1970s the eight hundred thousand Cuban immigrants living in the United States made up the largest group of post–World War II refugees in the nation. That began to change when the Vietnam War ended in 1973 and the American-backed regime in South Vietnam collapsed in 1975. When the Communists overran South Vietnam, those who had helped the Americans faced imprisonment or death. In March 1975 President Gerald Ford ordered the evacuation of any Vietnamese nationals and their dependents who had worked for the United States.

At the time the United States was undergoing a severe recession and many feared the Vietnamese would take American jobs. As a result, only 36 percent of the American public supported the resettle-

*Vietnamese refugees, also known as "boat people," attempting to flee the Communist regime of their war-torn homeland in the late 1970s.*

ment of the Vietnamese refugees. Despite the opposition, in 1975 the Ford administration used emergency funds to aid refugees and paroled 130,000. The next year Congress appropriated $450 million annually to provide housing, vocational training, medical care, language instruction, and social services to about 100,000 Vietnamese arriving in America every year.

In 1978 the situation in Southeast Asia grew worse as Communists took over Cambodia and Laos while hostilities erupted between Vietnam and China. This created a massive humanitarian crisis as tens of thousands of "boat people" tried to escape to neighboring countries by sea on makeshift, overcrowded, and often dangerous vessels. At the urging of the

United Nations High Commission for Refugees, U.S. navy ships began rescuing thousands of boat people. By 1979 the government was paroling 7,000 Southeast Asian boat people a month. By 1980 that number had doubled to 14,000.

## "Hardship for Refugees"

The majority of the Southeast Asian immigrants were poor, illiterate farmers from rural villages who relied on hunting and fishing to survive. Many experienced culture shock in the United States, as David M. Reimers writes in *Still the Golden Door: The Third World Comes to America:* "Differences over family structure and roles, work, leisure, religion, social and cultural customs, and life-style were often sharp, promoting misunderstanding by Americans and hardship for refu-

gees."[60] One widely reported example of misunderstanding occurred in 1980 when Vietnamese immigrants were accused of hunting pigeons, ducks, squirrels, and even stray dogs for food in San Francisco's Golden Gate Park.

Besides cultural differences, many Americans resented the billions of dollars the government spent to finance programs for the immigrants. In New Orleans black leaders complained that the Asians were being given benefits and favors denied to the city's African American population. As one unnamed American said: "The government gives them loans and houses but doesn't care about us."[61]

## Seeking Asylum

Even as the boat people struggled to establish themselves in an unfamiliar society, an-

---

# "We Don't Have a Country"

*Many of the Southeast Asian refugees who came to America between 1975 and 1985 were traumatized by war. Upon arrival in the United States, they suffered culture shock and prejudice. In* The Uprooted: Refugees in the United States, *an unnamed tenth-grade Cambodian boy describes his experiences at school:*

The Americans tell us to go back to our own country. I say we don't have a country to go back to. I wish I was born here and nobody would fight me and beat me up. They don't understand. I want to tell [them] if they had tried to cross the river [to escape Cambodia] and were afraid of being caught and killed, and lost their sisters, they might feel like me, they might look like me, and they, too, might find themselves in a new country.

Quoted in David M. Donahue and Nancy Flowers, *The Uprooted: Refugees in the United States.* Alameda, CA: Hunter House, 1995, p.127.

---

other group of people gained national attention with similar desperate escapes on the high seas. However, these people were not fleeing Communists, but escaping a repressive right-wing regime in Haiti.

Although secret police in Haiti jailed, tortured, and killed opponents, Haitians could not qualify as political refugees because their government had the political support of the United States. As such, Haitians fleeing political repression were simply treated as illegal aliens by the INS.

To gain asylum each Haitian had to prove that he or she had a "well-founded fear"[62] of persecution at home because of race, religion, or political opinion. Since the majority of Haitians were extremely poor and uneducated, most had a difficult time making their cases to immigration judges. Those who could not afford bail often sat in jail for months until they were deported.

The Haitian cause served as a catalyst for Congress to redefine the meaning of refugee. Senator Edward Kennedy (D-MA) wanted to move the designation away from "its present European and Cold War framework."[63] Meanwhile, other senators were unhappy with the repeated use of the president's parole powers, which were seen as a way of usurping Congress's authority over immigration.

To remedy these problems, Congress passed and president Jimmy Carter signed the Refugee Act in February 1980. The law enlarged to fifty thousand the number of refugees who would be admitted annually. The president could increase that number, but was required to ask approval of the Senate before he could do so. Finally, the term *refugee* was made to conform with the UN definition; that is, anyone who cannot return home for fear of persecution. The new law eliminated the terms "from Communist or Communist-dominated governments" as defined by the Refugee Relief Act of 1953.

One aspect of the 1980 Refugee Act was completely new. The law recognized the right of asylum to people who were already living in the United States. Defined by the term "asylee," these people came to the country on student or visitor visas and remained in the country illegally when the visas expired. Under terms of the bill, five thousand asylees could come forward and apply for permanent residence annually.

## Exceptions Were Made

Like most other immigrant bills in earlier years, the terms of the Refugee Act were ignored almost immediately. In April 1980, six weeks after the bill went into law, Fidel Castro announced that anyone who wanted to leave Cuba would be allowed to emigrate as long as he or she went to the United States. In Florida thousands of Cuban Americans promptly rented boats and headed to the port of Mariel, Cuba, to rescue their friends and relatives. This operation, known as the Mariel Boat Lift, brought one hundred twenty-five thousand Cubans to the United States within a month.

The Mariel immigrants were in violation of the Refugee Act, but Americans generally supported the exodus. As had happened before, exceptions were made for the refugees and most were allowed to remain in the United States.

*A boat packed with Cuban refugees lands at Florida's Key West naval base in April 1980 upon its return from Mariel, Cuba. The Mariel Boat Lift brought one hundred twenty-five thousand Cubans to the United States within a month in 1980.*

During the rest of the 1980s, the refugee crisis continued to grow. In 1987 a UN report estimated that due to wars and economic problems there were 13.3 million refugees worldwide. Because of the limitations of the Refugee Act most could not immigrate to the United States. Ironically, those who were in the country illegally could seek asylum and bypass those trying to enter legally from other nations. Whatever their situation, in the post–Vietnam War years, the United States remained a destination of choice for millions of refugees from nearly every continent on earth.

# Chapter Five

# Battles on the Border

Between 1965 and 1980 more than 10 million immigrants legally moved to the United States. Unlike the early decades of the century, when immigrants came mainly from Europe, the majority of the new immigrants were from impoverished nations in the developing world. Never before had the cultural makeup of the United States included so many Hispanics, Asians, Indian Asians, West Indians, Middle Easterners, and Africans. The remaking of American society could be traced to the relaxation of restrictions and quotas that followed the passage of the Immigration and Naturalization Services Act of 1965.

Many native-born Americans viewed the changes as positive and appreciated the contributions the new immigrants were making to society. But another aspect of immigration during this time was much less popular with the public. The attitude was summed up in a 1972 headline in *U.S. News & World Report*: "Surge of Illegal Immigrants Across American Borders: Never before have so many aliens swarmed illegally into U.S.—millions moving across nation."[64]

The article in *U.S. News & World Report* was among hundreds of anti-immigration articles that appeared in the media in the early 1970s. Stories inevitably featured photos of young men wading across the Rio Grande on the border or crowds of immigrants running through highway checkpoints in California, Arizona, New Mexico, or Texas. The tone set by the articles was often one of near panic and immigration was described as an alien invasion, an uncontrolled hemorrhage of people, and a costly nightmare.

Until this time, immigration issues had been largely ignored for several years. But the articles began to attract the public's attention. This changing situation set the tone for yet another drawn-out contentious debate about the role of immigrants in American society.

# Losing Control of the Borders

Whatever the popular views of immigration, the issue was gaining notice because of the sheer numbers of undocumented aliens entering the United States every year. Although it is impossible to calculate exact figures, the federal government estimates that in the 1970s and 1980s between 500,000 and 1.5 million people entered the United States illegally every year. About 80 percent of these people were from Mexico, but immigrants illegally entered the country from Central America, the Caribbean, and elsewhere as well.

As more people entered the country illegally, the number of people apprehended by the Border Patrol swelled. For example, in 1970 the Border Patrol arrested and deported 325,000 people. By 1980 that number had more than tripled to over 1 million.

Those who opposed this wave of immigration said that illegal immigrants were pushing down wages, taking jobs formerly held by poor Americans, and costing taxpayers billions for social services such as hospital care, schools, and police. Another common concern was expressed by prominent columnist Carl Rowan, who wrote in the *Cincinnati Enquirer:*

> The United States is a nation without meaningful control of its borders. So many Mexicans are crossing U.S. borders illegally that Mexicans are reclaiming Texas, California, and other territories that they have long claimed the Gringos stole from them.[65]

Those who disagreed with such assessments pointed out that immigrants had been contributing to society for many years and they performed tasks that benefited the majority of Americans. For example, because of the low wages paid to immigrant farmworkers, Americans had an abundant supply of cheap food. In addition, people were coming to America for the same reason Europeans immigrated earlier in the century, to make better lives for themselves and their children.

## A Wave of Resentment

While some sympathized with those arguments and defended increased immigration as a positive trend, the late 1970s saw a wave of resentment toward immigrants unlike any seen since the 1920s. A Roper poll from that time showed 80 percent of Americans wanted to reduce the number of legal immigrants and refugees entering the United States, and 91 percent supported an all-out effort to stop illegal immigration.

To deal with the growing concern, Congress created the Select Commission on Immigration and Refugee Policy in 1978. The commission's sixteen-member panel consisted of a group of immigration experts from the House of Representatives, the Senate, and presidential appointees and cabinet officials from the executive branch. One member, Pennsylvania Representative Joshua Eilberg , explained why immigration issues needed to be examined at that time:

*Suspected illegal immigrants are arrested on the U.S.-Mexico border.*

There is a paucity of hard data in this country on the impact of immigration, both legal and illegal. This is indeed disturbing when you consider that our immigration law has not been reviewed in over twenty-five years and that almost every aspect of the American community is affected by immigration. In my judgment, it is vital that every effort be made to reevaluate our immigration policy and that it be done in the comprehensive fashion.[66]

For several years the commission worked with federal agencies, immigration experts, and public interest groups to study every aspect of immigration. In March 1981 the commission issued a 435-page report. Although the sixty-seven recommendations in the report were wide ranging, it stated, "No policy issue received more attention from the Select Commission than that of illegal aliens—what to do about the presence of a large number of them in the United States and how to curtail future flows."[67]

## Opening and Closing Doors

The report stated that more immigrants could be admitted to the United States if illegal immigration were stopped, suggesting that the United States "close the back door to undocumented and illegal migration [and open] the front door a little more to accommodate legal migration."[68]

The Select Commission report recommended tough enforcement as a way to control immigration. Measures included adding more Border Patrol officers and cracking down on alien smugglers. There were also proposals to create civil and criminal penalties against employers who hired illegal immigrants: At the time, thirty-eight states had no laws against hiring illegal immigrants.

In a controversial move, the Select Commission suggested granting one-time amnesty to the 4 to 6 million illegal immigrants already in the United States before January 1980. Finally, commission adviser Philip L. Martin gave an important perspective to the issue:

> Immigration reform is a social issue that generates tension but defies an easy solution. Tension is reflected in the psychological feeling that the United States should curb immigration in an era of limits. The reality is that immigration is at an all-time high. If the United States cannot grope its way toward a consensus, it risks extreme, probably restrictionist action.[69]

## The Immigration Reform and Control Act

Wyoming senator Alan Simpson was a member of the Select Commission but did not support the conclusions of the report. Echoing the anti-immigrant sentiments of earlier times, Simpson wrote a letter to the *Washington Post* stating that illegal immigrants will "create in America some of the same social, political, and economic problems that exist in the countries from which they had chosen to depart. Furthermore . . . the unity and political stability of our nation will—in time—be seriously eroded."[70]

*Wyoming senator Alan Simpson influenced immigration policy by cosponsoring the Immigration Reform and Control Act of 1986.*

implementing a counterfeit-proof identification system for all workers.

The Simpson-Mazzoli bill parted with the commission when it mandated that relatives of legal immigrants be counted within the quota of five hundred forty thousand set for total immigration. It also removed preferences for brothers and sisters of U.S. citizens. By barring siblings and counting relatives under the quota, total immigration would be reduced.

## Favoring Agricultural Interests

The Simpson-Mazzoli bill was first introduced in 1981 but failed to pass. The bill was reintroduced every year thereafter until final passage was achieved. Formally known as the Immigration Reform and Control Act of 1986 (IRCA), the Simpson-Mazzoli bill contained four major provisions. The first part of the law shifted the burden of immigration enforcement away from the government onto employers. Under provisions of the act, employers could only hire workers who were native-born Americans, naturalized immigrants, or resident aliens. To ascertain their status, employers were required to examine an employee's passport, certificate of citizenship, Social Security card, birth certificate, driver's license,

As a powerful senator, Simpson was in a better position to influence immigration policy than the Select Commission. Working with a cosponsor, Kentucky representative Romano L. Mazzoli, Simpson introduced a bill to deal with immigration issues. The Simpson-Mazzoli bill adopted some recommendations from the Select Report such as improved border security and penalties for employers who hired illegal immigrants. The bill also proposed

# New Nativist Sentiments

*As the number of undocumented immigrants increased in the early 1990s, negative views about the newcomers were widespread. In 1994 journalist David Cole listed common stereotypes Americans held about illegal aliens as seen in the media and pubic opinion polls.*

From the enactment of [the Immigration Reform and Control Act of 1986] into the mid-1990s, the social construction of illegal aliens as an unsavory and very undesirable social element continued to take shape. In short time, illegal aliens ceased to be merely those who enter the country without proper documents. [In the public mind they] are the pregnant Mexican welfare cheat who crosses the border to San Diego to have babies . . . and in turn enable the mother to claim welfare benefits . . . the Mexican and Asian youth gangs contributing to urban crime problems; the single Hispanic men loitering on suburban street corners. . . . They are the children crowding into the urban public schools, demanding bilingual education and other special services . . . [and] the families without insurance who jam our public hospital emergency rooms.

David Cole, "Five Myths About Immigration," *Nation*, October 17, 1994, pp. 10–11.

state-issued ID, or other approved documents. Companies were then required to fill out a federal form for each employee hired and keep it on file in case INS inspectors ever requested it.

The new requirements were extremely unpopular with employers because the cost of creating, administering, and maintaining the files was estimated at $50,000 to $100,000 a year for large employers. This was seen as ludicrous since illegal aliens were able to buy fake Social Security cards and other documents on street corners for less than $50. Finally, opponents accused the system of unfairness— the law actually favored illegal aliens in the agricultural industry, they charged. As Daniels explains:

Everyone knows that agricultural employers in two states—California and Texas—have been hiring illegal aliens since the World War ll era and before. Since most of these are migrants who move from job to job, the only effective way for INS agents to apprehend those who have crossed the border has been to conduct raids on the fields at harvest time. Due to pressure from congresspersons representing grower interests, the new law specifically forbids INS agents from "interfering" with workers in the fields, although spot raids on places of urban employment, such as garment manufacturing shops, are still permitted.[71]

Besides lax enforcement, growers were allowed to request two hundred fifty thousand temporary visas, called green cards, for agricultural "guest workers." No other industry was afforded this advantage.

Another section of IRCA provided sanctions against employers who hired illegal aliens and included fines and prison sentences for repeat offenders. This too favored growers, since the INS found it almost impossible to obtain convictions in small communities against those who broke the law. As Daniels writes: "Juries in agricultural regions of California and the Southwest simply will not convict their friends and neighbors for hiring illegal aliens."[72]

Perhaps because of the inequities of the bill, the INS dedicated only 10 percent of its personnel to the task of monitoring workplaces.

## Amnesty for the Undocumented

The most controversial part of the Immigration Reform and Control Act concerned granting amnesty to 3.1 million illegal aliens who had lived continuously in the United States between 1982 and 1986. To eventually obtain citizenship,

*Illegal Mexican immigrants in 1988 filling out the amnesty application as dictated by the Immigration Reform and Control Act.*

applicants first had to file for permanent residency status. This had to be done within eighteen months of the bill's passage and applicants had to meet certain requirements that were often difficult to prove. They could have no criminal convictions and must test negative for AIDS. They had to prove that they had not collected welfare and show that they could converse in simple English. In addition, each applicant had to pass a test on U.S. history and culture. If these requirements were not met, amnesty was repealed and the applicant was again an illegal alien subject to deportation.

## "Criminals, Welfare Cheats, and Freeloaders"

While several million aliens worked to gain amnesty, the law did little to stop hundreds of thousands more illegal immigrants from moving to the United States every year. As their numbers increased, public opinion hardened against all immigration. Every poll from that era shows at least 70 percent of Americans supported tough new immigration restrictions. As Evelyn Hu-DeHart writes in "Race, Civil Rights, and the New Immigrants: Nativism and the New World Order," illegal aliens were largely viewed as "criminals, welfare cheats, and freeloaders, social burdens who exacerbate our urban crime problem and severely strain the public resources that our taxes support."[73]

This extreme view of immigrants did not conform with reality. In fact, the 1990s census showed that only 8 percent of the total U.S. population was foreign born, about half the percentage of 1900. And af-

ter the amnesty program, only 13 percent of those people, or 2.5 million, were in the country illegally. In fact, illegal immigrants only accounted for 1 percent of the total population.

About one-third of the undocumented aliens were from Mexico, another third from Central America and the Caribbean, and the rest were from Europe, Canada, and Asia. The majority did not sneak over the border but entered the country legally and overstayed their visas.

## Liberalization and Political Backlash

Using these statistics as a guide, Congress decided to increase immigration despite public attitudes. The Immigration Act of 1990 raised the annual immigration ceiling to 700,000 for every year until 1994, at which time the ceiling dropped to 675,000 a year.

The Immigration Act also sought to solve problems in America's impoverished inner cities and countryside. Ten thousand permanent resident visas were offered to those who would promise to invest at least $1 million in U.S. urban areas or $500,000 in rural areas. In a final move, Congress repealed the provisions of the McCarran-Walters Act of 1952, which had banned immigrants because of their past political beliefs, statements, and associations.

Most immigrant organizations supported the new changes in the law. However, opponents viewed the Immigration Act as a brazen defiance of widespread public opinion. As activist Raul Yzaquirre commented: "Congress was clearly more liberal than the public."[74]

# "Abuse of Immigration Laws"

*In his State of the Union address in January 1995, President Bill Clinton mentioned immigration issues that were of concern to the majority of Americans:*

All Americans, not only in the states most heavily affected, but in every place in this country, are rightly disturbed by the large numbers of illegal aliens entering our country. The jobs they hold might otherwise be held by citizens or legal immigrants. The public services they use impose burdens on our taxpayers. That's why our administration has moved aggressively to secure our borders more by hiring a record number of new border guards, by deporting twice as many criminal aliens as ever before, by cracking down on illegal hiring, by barring welfare benefits to illegal aliens.

[We] will try to do more to speed the deportation of illegal aliens who are arrested for crimes, to better identify illegal aliens in the workplace. . . .

We are a nation of immigrants. But we are also a nation of laws. It is wrong and ultimately self-defeating for a nation of immigrants to permit the kind of abuse of our immigration laws we have seen in recent years, and we must do more to stop it.

William J. Clinton, "State of the Union 1995—Delivered Version," *From Revolution to Reconstruction,* March 6, 2003. http://odur.let.rug.nl/~usa/P/bc42/speeches/sud95wjc.htm.

*President Bill Clinton in 1995.*

To voice their unhappiness, those who opposed the liberalized law formed anti-immigrant grassroots groups across the nation. These groups gave interviews in the media, held meetings and rallies, and supported political candidates who held their views.

## A Political Cause

Not wanting to alienate the important anti-immigrant constituency, politicians of both major parties took up their political cause. They began blaming a host of social problems on illegal immigrants and proposing ways to deny them entry into the United States.

In 1992 conservative presidential candidate Pat Buchanan proposed building an impassable "Berlin Wall" on the U.S.-Mexico border like the one the Soviet Union erected to prevent citizens from escaping from East Germany between 1961 and 1989. Two years later in California, Pete Wilson was reelected governor with analysts attributing his victory to a strong anti-immigrant stance.

Anti-immigrant politicians also won gubernatorial races in Texas and Florida

*In the 1990s the anti-immigration issue was a hot topic for politicians. Here, running for president in 1996 Pat Buchanan speaks to the media at a section of the U.S.-Mexico border fence south of San Diego in 1996.*

and congressional races throughout the South. Political consultant Mark McKinnon analyzed the situation: "Immigration is a potential powder keg kind of issue. It plays to the politics of fear, and the politics of fear can be very persuasive."[75]

## "Save Our State"

Nothing illustrated McKinnon's point better than an initiative that was on the California ballot in November 1994. Called Proposition 187, or "Save Our State" (SOS), the measure was written to deny illegal immigrants a range of publicly funded services, including primary and secondary education. Illegal immigrants enrolled in California schools would be expelled immediately. Prop 187, as it was known, would also deny illegal immigrants nonemergency medical care and police assistance.

A particularly controversial measure of Prop 187 required public officials to act as informants for the government. It obligated teachers, school administrators, doctors, health care workers, and social workers to report anyone suspected of being an illegal immigrant to the INS.

Prop 187 was widely condemned by those who believed the measure was mean-spirited, racist, and divisive. They backed their beliefs buy touting a comprehensive study conducted by the Urban Institute of Washington, D.C., that showed most undocumented immigrants lived in fear of being discovered and deported. As a result, they were not likely to use social services and even if they tried to, they were ineligible for most.

By studying records of the 1986 amnesty program, the Urban Institute showed that less than 1 percent of those who sought naturalization had received government benefits. These included workers' compensation, unemployment insurance, and Supplemental Security Income (a program for older and disabled people). In addition, less than half of 1 percent received food stamps or welfare. Commenting on these statistics in a New York Times editorial, Frank Sharry of the pro-immigrant National Immigration Forum concluded: "These figures make clear that undocumented immigrants are not the burden on our country that [opponents portray] them as being, nor is illegal immigration so great a problem as [they state]."[76]

Despite Sharry's argument, Prop 187 passed with about 59 percent of the vote. However, the law was immediately challenged in court. Lawyers for various pro-immigrant groups questioned the constitutionality of Prop 187 since immigration is ruled by federal, not state, laws. In 1998 the challengers won and Prop 187, having never gone into effect, was overturned in federal court.

## Operation Gatekeeper

Even while Californians were debating Proposition 187 before the 1994 election, the federal government was taking steps to rein in illegal immigration. In September 1994 attorney general Janet Reno appeared in Los Angeles and, with great fanfare, announced a new program called Operation Gatekeeper. This program was initiated to tighten up security along the 5 miles (8.1km) of the westernmost border between San Diego County and Tijuana, Mexico.

Operation Gatekeeper was a response to a common problem in this region. On many nights, migrants would gather in large groups in Tijuana and make a dash for the border. While some were apprehended as they ran past U.S. checkpoints on the highway, hundreds were able to escape the overwhelmed Border Patrol.

This scene provided enough drama to attract news cameras. Videos of the border crashers began to regularly appear on television and further enraged those opposed to illegal immigration.

To stop these highly publicized incidents, Operation Gatekeeper had the Border Patrol shift its emphasis from apprehension of migrants to deterrence. Dozens of new agents were put into high-visibility, fixed positions along the border. They were backed by a three-layered defense system of agents who could apprehend those who made it past the past the first line of defense. The border station also received new equipment from the Department of Defense, including four-wheel-drive vehicles, infrared night scopes, and motion sensors.

Within days Operation Gatekeeper drastically reduced illegal immigration in the region and the program was declared a great success by the Border Patrol and the INS.

## Traveling with Coyotes

But reducing illegal immigration in the Operation Gatekeeper region did not stop illegal immigration elsewhere. As soon as the program went into effect, migration routes shifted eastward, into rugged undeveloped terrain where the patrols had

not been reinforced. With new obstacles placed before the migrants, many began sneaking into the country aided by guides known as coyotes. These men specialized in guiding migrants past the Border Patrol and across busy highways, rivers, railroad tracks, and over dangerous mountains. For their services, coyotes charged migrants about $100 to escort them just over the border to San Diego and $300 for a ride to Los Angeles in the trunk of a car. Those wishing to fly to

*Surveillance cameras, monitored by the U.S. Border Patrol, posted along the U.S.-Mexico border in Calexico, California.*

Chicago paid the coyote $1,000. These fees were all-inclusive and covered transportation, food, and accommodations in a network of safe houses.

With such large sums to be made, the coyote business grew quickly. According to immigration experts, by 1996 the coyote business was a $350 million a year industry. This made it the fourth largest enterprise along the border after tourism, commerce, and the factory assembly businesses run by large corporations such as General Motors and Sony.

To slow the continual flow of migrants, the government instituted phase two of Operation Gatekeeper in October 1995. An immigration court was established directly on the border to process

# The Coyote and the Robber

*Danger always lurks along the Mexico border for those who attempt to cross illegally. In* Mexican Voices/American Dreams, *Marilyn P. Davis describes the coyotes and robbers (coyotes and rateros) working the border:*

El coyote is a specialist in eluding, avoiding, skirting around, fading away from and passing over, the trials of the border. The more difficult the border becomes, the more in demand are his services. And, despite the high cost of being taken across, people keep migrating. . . .

But ballooning demand and big money bring out *el coyote's* counterpart, *el ratero* [the robber]. *El ratero* always passes himself off as *el coyote*. *El ratero* is as easy to find as *el coyote* is difficult. . . . Barking his pitch at the bus station as people disembark from the interior provinces, or speaking in [a quiet voice] along border approaches to catch those just turned back, he promises, "With me it's secure." If they believe him, they will surely lose their money and maybe their lives. He may be small-time, operating alone, or part of a mafia-type crime family trafficking in drugs or prostitution and backed by paid-off police. Anything is possible at the border and becomes increasingly probable as people bring more and more money to buy their way across.

Marilyn P. Davis, *Mexican Voices/American Dreams.* New York: Henry Holt, 1990, p. 128.

and deport those who tried to enter the country with counterfeit documents. The government also implemented a new computerized system, called IDENT, to identify aliens who repeatedly tried to enter the United States as well as those with criminal records.

## Illegal Immigration Reform

In September 1996 the government continued its crackdown on illegal aliens when President Bill Clinton signed into law the Illegal Immigration Reform and Immigrant Responsibility Act of 1996 (IIRIRA). This law was extremely complicated and contained over six hundred sections that covered countless esoteric aspects of legal and illegal immigration.

The IIRIRA increased the INS budget by 24 percent and authorized hiring five thousand new border agents before 2001, a move that doubled the size of the Border Patrol. The act also defined a host of new crimes and added monetary penalties for violators. For example, the fine for illegally crossing into the United States was set at a maximum of $250, a fortune to someone commonly making $3 a day. Those migrants who attempted to evade law enforcement checkpoints at high speeds would be subject to imprisonment for up to five years.

The IIRIRA also affected the thousands of legal immigrants who crossed the border every day, many of whom lived in one country and commuted to jobs in another. These people were now required to carry new border crossing identification cards with "biometric identifiers" such as fingerprints or handprints. A new computerized system was put into place to match the number of departures with the number of entries into the United States. Those who entered but did not leave would be pursued by INS agents.

To deal with the coyote issue, a new task force of six hundred personnel was formed to investigate alien smuggling. This team would also investigate the unlawful employment of aliens and search for those who overstayed their visas. After the IIRIRA was passed Clinton signed an executive order that excluded companies from doing business with the federal government if they knowingly hired illegal immigrants.

In conjunction with the IIRIRA, Congress passed the Personal Responsibility and Work Opportunity Reconciliation Act, also known as the welfare reform bill. While this law mainly dealt with U.S. citizens collecting welfare, provisions of the act cut many social programs for immigrants. For example, legal immigrants lost their right to food stamps and Supplemental Security Income. Illegal immigrants become ineligible for any federal benefits except emergency medical care, immunization programs, and disaster relief.

## The Triple Fence

The most visible aspect of the IIRIRA was the construction of a nearly impenetrable 14-mile-long (22.5km) barrier from the Pacific Ocean to the Otay Mountains east of San Diego. The barrier, known as the triple fence, was built by National Guard units at a cost of $42 million.

As the name suggests, the triple fence consists of three fences. The first is solid steel and 11 feet (3.4m) high. A second fence is a 15-foot (4.6m) steel construction that is angled toward Mexico. The third is a concrete fence 15 feet (4.6m) high, also angled toward Mexico. Between each fence is a cleared area between 100 and 500 feet (30.5m to 152m) wide. This is a security zone where migrants trapped between the fences can be apprehended. The area is lit twenty-four hours a day and is under constant remote control video surveillance in addition to manned patrols.

By all accounts the triple fence did less to curb illegal immigration than to force illegal immigrants east into the extremely rugged terrain of the Otay Mountains and the desert beyond them. Neither the mountain peaks (as high as 6,000 feet (1,829m) nor extreme temperatures (below freezing six months of the year in the mountains, and as high as 120°F (48.9°C) in the desert in summer) have deterred people from attempting to cross the border by these dangerous eastern routes.

## Migrant Deaths

After the triple fence was completed, the number of deaths occurring during illegal border crossings climbed over 600 percent. Each year, according to the Border

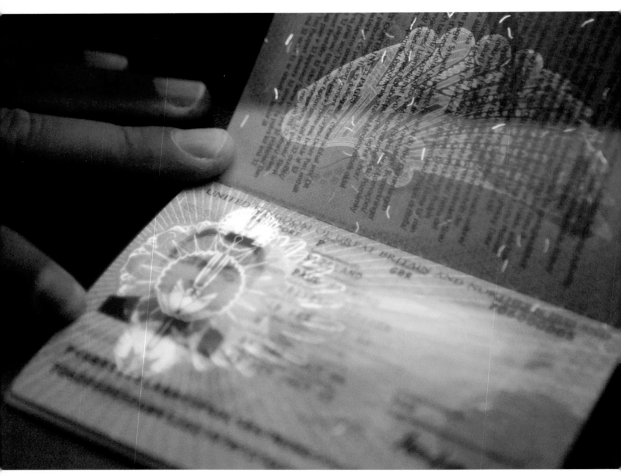

*Biometric passports contain computer chips that can store data such as the fingerprints or handprints of the passport holder.*

Patrol, between three hundred and four hundred people die from heat stroke, dehydration, and hypothermia trying to cross into the United States.

The triple fence also empowered coyotes. The new routes around the fence require immigrants to walk two or three days through extreme terrain and deadly weather conditions. Often they are unprepared for such an arduous journey, wearing only street shoes and carrying little water or food. Those who fail to keep up with their group might be left behind to die. These desolate desert routes are also populated with drug traffickers and other assorted criminals who rape, rob, or murder migrants. Migrants who survive the walk are packed into vans with no heat or air conditioning. These vehicles have been involved in dozens of accidents and hundreds have died as drivers try to outrun the Border Patrol.

Despite the dangers, it quickly became evident that Operation Gatekeeper was doing little to slow illegal immigration. Although the number of apprehensions by the Border Patrol in the San Diego region dropped about 80 percent, the total number of migrants arrested along the border as a whole remained about the same.

## The Argument Remains the Same

As in previous years, the new laws did little to change the reality of U.S. immigration. Those living in dire poverty or under harsh political repression continue to risk their lives to come to America, as they have done for centuries.

In the years since the first immigrants walked through Ellis Island, much has changed in the United States. With its automobiles, highways, televisions, computers, and other modern technology the nation would barely be recognizable to an immigrant from 1900. However, if that immigrant read a modern newspaper, he or she would recognize one thing that has not changed much in the past century. People continue to argue, often vociferously, over the role of immigrants and immigration. The arguments have changed very little even as the United States remains the primary destination for the poor and oppressed people throughout the world.

# Notes

## Introduction: Modern Immigration: Benefit or Burden?

1. Maldwyn Allen Jones, *American Immigration.* Chicago: University of Chicago Press, 1965, p. 249.
2. Quoted in Virginia Yans-McLaughlin and Marjorie Lightman, *Ellis Island and the Peopling of America.* New York: New Press, 1997, p. 10.
3. Quoted in Joan Morrison and Charlotte Fox Zabusky, *American Mosaic: The Immigrant Experience in the Words of Those Who Lived It.* New York: E.P. Dutton, 1980, p. 9.
4. Quoted in Marian L. Smith, "Overview of INS History," U.S. Citizenship and Immigration Service, January 20, 2006. www.uscis.gov/graphics/about us/history/articles/oview. htm.
5. Quoted in Smith, "Overview of INS History."
6. Quoted in John Higham, *Strangers in the Land.* New York: Atheneum, 1981, p. 23.

## Chapter 1: The Ellis Island Years

7. Yans-McLaughlin and Lightman, *Ellis Island and the Peopling of America,* p. 59.
8. Quoted in Willard A. Heaps, *The Story of Ellis Island.* New York: Seabury, 1967, p. 37.
9. National Park Service, "Ellis Island: History," Ellis Island Foundation, 2000. www.ellisisland.org/genealogy/ellis_island_history.asp.
10. Quoted in Heaps, *The Story of Ellis Island,* p. 75.
11. Quoted in Yans-McLaughlin and Lightman, *Ellis Island and the Peopling of America,* p. 66.
12. Quoted in Yans-McLaughlin and Lightman, *Ellis Island and the Peopling of America,* pp. 66-67.
13. Quoted in Andrew Dolkart, "The 1901 Tenement House Act, Part One: Birth of a Housing Act," 2006. www.tenement.org/features_dolkart2.html.
14. Quoted in Higham, *Strangers in the Land,* p. 172.
15. Higham, *Strangers in the Land,* p. 165.
16. Jones, *American Immigration,* p. 267.
17. Quoted in Jones, *American Immigration,* p. 268.
18. Theodore Roosevelt, "Theodore Roosevelt Advocates Americanism, 1915," *Proud to Be an American,* 2002. www.rpatrick.com/USA/americanism.

## Chapter 2: Closing the Doors

19. Quoted in Nancy Russell, "Henry Ford: American Anti-Semitism and the Class Struggle," *World Socialist,* April 18, 2003. www.wsws.org/articles/2003/apr2003/ford-a18_prn.shtml.
20. Higham, *Strangers in the Land,* p. 227.
21. Quoted in Dale T. Knobel, *America for the Americans: The Nativist Movement*

*in the United States.* New York: Twayne, 1996, p. 257.

22. Quoted in Jon Winoker, "Curmudgeon," *Funny Times,* November 2006, p. 4.

23. Quoted in "Fears of Dissent," *Between the Wars,* 2005. http://chnm.gmu.edu/courses/hist409/palmer.html.

24. Henry Ford, "The International Jew," *Anti-Defamation League,* 2006. www.jewishvirtuallibrary.org/jsource/antisemitism/ford.html.

25. Quoted in "The Klan Rides Again," *Between the Wars,* 2005. http://chnm.gmu.edu/courses/hist409/klan.html.

26. Quoted in Knobel, *America for the Americans,* p. 266.

27. Quoted in Higham, *Strangers in the Land,* p. 309.

28. Jones, *American Immigration,* p. 273.

## Chapter 3: Years of Isolation

29. Department of State, *Press Releases 3,* September 13, 1930, pp. 176–77.

30. Quoted in *Congressional Record,* June 26, 1935, p. 10,229.

31. Robert A. Divine, *American Immigration Policy, 1924–1952.* New Haven, CT: Yale University Press, 1957, p. 93.

32. Quoted in *Proceedings of the 53d Annual Convention of the AFL,* 1933. New York: The Committee, p. 103.

33. Quoted in *Congressional Record,* March 28, 1938, p. 4,227.

34. "State Department Press Release," *Interior Releases, 17,* December 20, 1940, p. 422.

35. Divine, *American Immigration Policy,* p. 104.

36. Roger Daniels, *Coming to America.* New York: HarperCollins, 1990, p. 296.

37. Thomas Archdeacon, *Becoming American: An Ethnic History.* New York: Free Press, 1983, p. 194.

38. Quoted in "The Politics," The Japanese-American Internment, February 3, 1997. www.geocities.com/Athens/8420/generations.html.

39. Kitty Calavita, *Inside the State.* New York: Routledge, 1992, p. 1.

40. *Migratory Labor in American Agriculture.* Washington, DC: Government Printing Office, 1951, p. 20.

41. *Migratory Labor in American Agriculture.* Washington, DC: Government Printing Office, 1951, p. 65.

42. Quoted in Calavita, *Inside the State,* p. 32.

43. Quoted in Calavita, *Inside the State,* p. 33.

## Chapter 4: Opening the Doors

44. Quoted in Stuart D. Stein, "Statements by Hitler and Senior Nazis Concerning Jews and Judaism," *The Jewish Holocaust,* March 4, 2000. www.ess.uwe.ac.uk/genocide/statements.htm.

45. Daniels, *Coming to America,* p. 329.

46. Nathan Glazer, ed., *Clamor at the Gates.* San Francisco: Institute for Contemporary Studies, 1985, p. 5.

47. Divine, *American Immigration Policy,* p. 146.

48. Patrick McCarran, *Congressional Record,* June 27, 1952, p. 8,267.

49. Quoted in Nicholas Capaldi, ed., *Immigration.* Amherst, NY: Prometheus, 1997, p. 125.

50. Harry Truman, *Congressional Record,* June 25, 1952, p. 8,083.

51. Patrick McCarran, *Congressional Record,* March 2, 1953, p. 1,518.

52. Quoted in "Document #328; July 20, 1953," The Presidential Papers of Dwight David Eisenhower, 2006. www.eisenhowermemorial.org/presidentialpapers/first-term/documents/328.cfm.

53. Quoted in Capaldi, *Immigration,* p. 126.
54. Quoted in Capaldi, *Immigration,* p. 127.
55. Quoted in Capaldi, *Immigration,* p. 120.
56. Otis L. Graham Jr., *Unguarded Gates.* Lanham, MD: Rowman & Littlefield, 2004, p.88.
57. Glazer, *Clamor at the Gates,* p. 6.
58. Quoted in Daniels, *Coming to America,* p. 340.
59. Quoted in Daniels, *Coming to America,* p. 341.
60. David M. Reimers, *Still the Golden Door: The Third World Comes to America.* New York: Columbia University Press, 1985, p 183.
61. Quoted in Reimers, *Still the Golden Door,* p. 184.
62. Quoted in U.S. Congress, "Haitian Immigrants," *Report of the House Subcommittee on Immigration, Citizenship, and International Law of the Committee on the Judiciary,* 94th Congress, p. 1.
63. Quoted in Reimers, *Still the Golden Door,* p. 190.

## Chapter 5: Battles on the Border

64. "Surge of Illegal Immigrants Across American Borders," *U.S. News & World Report,* January 17, 1972, pp. 32-33.
65. Quoted in Daniels, *Coming to America,* p. 390.
66. U.S. House, Representative Eilberg (PA), "Select Commission on Immigration and Refugee Policy," *Congressional Record,* 95th Congress, 18 July, 1978: H6854.
67. "Select Commission on Immigration and Refugee Policy." Washington, DC: Select Commission, 1981, Appendix E, p. 5.
68. Quoted in Philip L. Martin, "Select Commission Suggests Changes in Immigration Policy: A Review Essay," *Monthly Labor Review,* February 1982, p. 31.
69. Martin, "Select Commission Suggests Changes in Immigration Policy," p. 37.
70. Alan Simpson, editorial, *Washington Post,* April 28, 1981.
71. Daniels, *Coming to America,* p. 395.
72. Daniels, *Coming to America,* p. 396.
73. Evelyn Hu-DeHart, "Race, Civil Rights, and the New Immigrants: Nativism and the New World Order," *Ethnic Studies Journal,* 1997. www.colorado.edu/EthnicStudies/ethnicstudiesjournal/archive/Volume%20I%201/Civil%20Rights.html .
74. Quoted in Graham, *Unguarded Gates,* p. 154.
75. Quoted in Richard Berke, "Politicians Discovering an Issue: Immigration," *New York Times,* March 9, 1994, p. A14.
76. Frank Sharry, *New York Times,* September 1, 1993, p. A10.

# Glossary

**amnesty:** A pardon issued to those who have committed crimes, such as illegally entering the United States.

**citizen:** Someone who has a right to live in a country either through being born there or having obtained citizenship through legal channels.

**communism:** A totalitarian political and economic system based on the belief that the wealth and resources of a nation belong equally to all of its citizens.

**emigrant:** Someone who leaves his or her native country to live in another country.

**green card:** An identity card and work permit issued by the U.S. government to noncitizens.

**illegal alien:** In the United States, someone who lives and works in the country without a green card or other government-issued residence papers.

**immigrant:** Someone who has entered a country and permanently resides there.

**nativism:** The belief of native-born Americans who can trace their heritage to northern European nations that they are superior to more recent immigrants and immigrants from other parts of the world.

**parole:** Residency status granted by the government, often for humanitarian purposes, to people who do not meet the technical requirements for immigration.

**quota:** The maximum number of people allowed to immigrate from specific nations or political backgrounds.

**refugee:** Someone involuntarily forced to leave his or her native land because of war or persecution.

**resident alien:** A legal immigrant residing in the United States who has not obtained legal citizenship.

**steerage:** Third-class passenger accommodations on a ship, the cheapest method of travel, usually in the area of a ship's rudder and steering gear.

**visa:** An official endorsement in a passport that allows the holder to enter, leave, or freely travel through a particular country.

**xenophobia:** An intense fear or dislike of foreigners, their customs, and culture.

# For Further Reading

## Books

Sonia Benson, *U.S. Immigration and Migration Almanac.* Detroit: UXL/Thomson Gale, 2004. A comprehensive overview of the groups of people who have immigrated to the United States from various nations.

Meg Greene, *Polish Americans.* San Diego: Lucent Books/Thomson Gale, 2004. An exploration of the reasons millions of Poles immigrated to America, what their passage was like, the kinds of jobs they found, the communities they formed, and the discrimination they faced.

Miranda Hunter, *Latino Americans and Immigration Laws: Crossing the Border.* Philadelphia: Mason Crest, 2006. A study of immigration law and policy, the reasons Latinos migrate to the United States, and issues of legal and illegal immigration.

Michael Kerrigan, *Border and Immigration Control.* Broomall, PA: Mason Crest, 2003. Issues of immigration and security along the southern border of the United States.

Marissa Lingen, *The Jewish Americans.* Broomall, PA: Mason Crest, 2003. Discusses the early-twentieth-century influx of Jews from eastern Europe, the American response to the Holocaust and Jewish refugees, and important Jewish immigrants and Jewish Americans.

Lisa Trumbauer, *Russian Immigrants.* New York: Facts On File, 2005. Interesting discussion of the historical reasons why Russians have immigrated to the United States.

## Web Sites

"The Japanese Internment," C. John Yu, June 18, 2006. www.geocities.com/Athens/8420/main.html. A site dealing with the internment of Japanese immigrants during World War II with links to photos, informative essays, related Web sites, and more.

"The Red Scare: 1919–1920," U-S-History.com, 2005. www.u-s-history.com/pages/h1343.html. Information about the Red Scare that resulted in the deportation of thousands of immigrants in the 1920s era of anti-Communist hysteria.

"U.S. Policy During World War II," Jewish Virtual Library, 2006. www.jewishvirtuallibrary.org/jsource/Holocaust/us_pol.html. Links to documents and Web sites dealing with government policies concerning Jewish immigrants, refugees, and others.

William Williams, "Ellis Island Photographs from the Collection of William Williams, Commissioner of Immigration, 1902–1913," NYPL Gallery, 2004. http://digitalgallery.nypl.org/nypldigital/explore/dgexplore.cfm?topic=culture&collection_list=EllisIslandPhotograp&col_id=165. Eighty-three photographs relating to Ellis Island and immigration to the United States in the early twentieth century published on a Web site hosted by the New York City Public Library.

# Index

Czolgosz, Leon, 21

Daniels, Roger
   on illegal agricultural workers, 82, 83
   on pre-World War II refugee policy, 51, 63
Daughters of the American Revolution, 30
Davis, Marilyn P., 90
*Dearborn Independent* (newspaper), 31, 35–36
De Carli, Bianca, 14
deportations, 17, 33, 66
Dickstein, Samuel, 47–48
Dies, Martin, 47
displaced persons, 64–65
Displaced Persons Act (1948), 64–65
Divine, Robert A., 42
   on asylum, 47, 51
   on immigration laws, 65
drying-out policy, 59
Duncan, Marion Moncure, 70

economy
   agricultural workers and, 56, 58–61
   business opposition to quotas, 39–41
   Great Depression, 45–47
   illegal immigrants and, 78, 91
   need for immigrant labor, 35
   Roaring Twenties, 28, 44
   *see also* labor
Eilberg, Joshua, 78, 80
Eisenhower, Dwight D., 67
Ellis Island, 12–13, 14–17
*Ellis Island and the People of America* (Yans-
   McLaughlin and Lightman), 12
Emergency Quota Act (1921), 39–41
enemy aliens, 51–56, 70
ethnic communities, 17–19, 28, 34
eugenics, 24, 41
Evans, Hiram Wesley, 36
Executive Order 9066, 52–56

family members
   Congressional petitions for, 68
   effect of entry refusal, 16
   priority under quotas for, 42–43, 66
   restrictions on, 81
   reunification visas, 71, 72
Farmers National Congress, 30
farmworkers, 56, 58–61, 78, 82–83
Federal Bureau of Investigation (FBI), 32, 51
*Federal Textbook on Citizenship,* 44
Florida, 86
Ford, Gerald, 72, 73
Ford, Henry
   anti-Semitism of, 35–36
   automobile factory, 19–20
   on Communists, 31

   English classes and, 26
Ford Motor Company, 19–20, 31, 36
442nd Regimental Combat Team, 55–56
Frowne, Sadie, 19

General Motors, 20
German Americans during World War I, 25–27
German immigrants
   Operation Paperclip and, 69
   preferential treatment of, 42, 64, 65–66, 67
   during World War I, 25–27
   during World War II, 51
Glazer, Nathan, 64, 71
Goldman, Emma, 33, 35
Graham, Otis L., Jr., 70
Grant, Madison, 24
Great Depression, 45–47, 48
green cards, 83
Guernsey, Mrs. George Thacher, 30
guest workers, 83

Haitian immigrants, 75
Harding, Warren G., 39
health of immigrants, 13–15, 18
Heartbreak Island. *See* Ellis Island
Higham, John, 23, 30, 32
history, 8–10
Hitler, Adolf, 36, 47, 63
Holocaust, 63
Hoover, Herbert, 46–47
Hoover, J. Edgar, 32
Hu-DeHart, Evelyn, 84
hyphenated Americans, 22, 25–26

IDENT system, 91
illegal immigrants
   amnesty for, 80, 83–84
   asylum for, 75, 76
   bracero program and, 59–61
   coyotes and rateros, 88–89, 90
   number of (1970-1990), 78
   penalties for, 90–91
   percent of U.S. population (1990), 84
   public debate about, 77, 78, 80, 84–87
   services to, 87, 91
   triple fence and, 91–92
Illegal Immigration Reform and Immigrant
   Responsibility Act (IIRIRA, 1996), 90–91
immigrants
   average number processed at Ellis Island
     annually, 13
   federal benefits for, 91
   number of (1880-1900), 9–10
   number of (1900-1920), 17
   number of (1965-1980), 72, 77
   unregulated, 8

# Picture Credits

# About the Author

Stuart A. Kallen is the author of more than two hundred nonfiction books for children and young adults. He has written on subjects ranging from the theory of relativity to the history of rock and roll. He has also written award-winning children's videos and television scripts. In his spare time, Kallen is a singer/songwriter/guitarist in San Diego, California.